There was a child who was so mild
That no one thought of her as wild.
And yet beneath her gentle face
Was chaos time could not erase.

And every day her pain would stay
Just out of reach, in no one's way.
And though she smiled, her soul was riled
Because it had been long defiled.

Yet, unreleased, her pain increased
Until her deepest longings ceased.
And in her mind she built the kind
Of fortress no one else could find.

Now all alone, in walls of stone,
A young girl guards her fragile throne.
And nobody can hurt her there,
And nobody can show they care.

So pain presumptuously plods on
With fear the queen and rage the pawn.
They fight to shield and yet to free
The little girl I once called Me.

Front cover and poem
by
Linda Price

Multiple Identities

Understanding and Supporting the Severely Abused

by

Diane W. Hawkins, M.A.

Published by

Restoration in Christ Ministries

PO Box 479, Grottoes, VA 24441-0479

540-249-9119; Fax 540-249-9716

www.rcm-usa.org

2nd revised and expanded edition
Originally published as
Supporting Ritual Abuse Survivors

ISBN 0-9708073-3-3
Library of Congress Control Number: 2001126138

Printed in the U.S.A.
by
Morris Publishing
3212 E. Hwy. 30
Kearney, NE 68847
1-800-650-7888
Fax 308-237-0263

The author is not a mental health practitioner. No diagnosis or treatment protocol should be established solely on the basis of this book. Any application of the recommendations given is at the readers's discretion and sole risk. No guarantee of outcome is made.

Dedication

With love and appreciation
to my beloved husband
and greatest supporter,

Tom

Table of Contents

Table of Figures

Preface

As a ritual abuse survivor with a diagnosis of Dissociative Identity Disorder (DID), I am personally acquainted with the realities of severe abuse and dissociation as well as the complex dynamics which make the journey to recovery so long and oftentimes so lonely. Too often the diagnosis of DID leads to a tremendous sense of isolation in a world that has no "box" in which to fit us. Building any kind of a relationship usually requires that we live behind an artificial mask, trying our best to conceal the dynamics of who we really are and the struggles that are so real in our lives.

This book is an effort on my part to help bridge this information gap, bringing understanding that will hopefully result in greater support for those who are courageously fighting to reclaim lives shattered by unspeakable evil. I have drawn its contents not only from my personal experience but also from my observations and interactions with scores of other abuse survivors whom I have met in various types of therapy groups as well as through my involvement with Restoration in Christ Ministries, an organization devoted to addressing the needs of dissociated survivors of severe abuse.

I have chosen to use the feminine gender throughout the book simply for the purpose of smoother reading. While the majority of abuse survivors seeking healing are indeed female, in actual fact males are victims of early childhood abuse resulting in DID just as frequently. They are just less apt to acknowledge it and seek treatment.

Because I am a Christian and God is such an integral part of my life, I cannot help but write from a Christian perspective. I have also experienced the dramatic effects of bringing God into the healing process. I believe that He is absolutely necessary to resolving the spiritual dynamics present when Satanic Ritual Abuse (SRA) is involved. While I tend to address my audience as fellow-Christians, many of the psychological dynamics and humanitarian needs I describe in connection with abuse survivors will be helpful to all, whether Christian or not.

I originally designed the book to bring understanding and guidance to current and potential supporters of ritual abuse survivors. However, while it is written to include the more complex dynamics of these particular survivors, much of the material applies to survivors of other forms of abuse as well. Furthermore, it has also proven to be extremely instructive and affirming to survivors themselves, especially in the early stages of therapy.

Appendix A contains a glossary of terms which are commonly associated with Dissociative Identity Disorder (DID) and ritual abuse and is designed to assist those readers to whom these phenomena are relative new. I urge you to consult it whenever you encounter unfamiliar terminology and particularly draw your attention to my definitions of "cult" and "cultist," which I use in a slightly uncustomary way in this book.

I trust that you will find the book helpful in understanding the issues and needs of deeply wounded people, whether that is yourself or someone you know. As understanding and acceptance continue to grow, survivors can emerge from the shadows and more readily receive the help and support they so desperately need.

Acknowledgments

I want to express my deep appreciation to Linda Price for the use of her artwork on the cover, as well as her accompanying poem, and to Sheila Salmon for the cover layout design. Many thanks also go to Dr. Scott Moose and Juli Kuhl for their gracious advisory help in proofreading most of the manuscript. Juli also helped significantly in encouraging me to publish the book without it reaching my own standard of perfection so that the information can get out.

I also owe tremendous gratitude to the many therapists, primary and otherwise, who have guided and supported me along my own therapeutic journey, enabling me now to be of assistance to others so that their journey is not quite as mysterious and lonely as my own. Dr. Dennis Bull bravely tackled the beginning years of my therapy, confirming my diagnosis and guiding me through what were extremely turbulent, and largely uncharted, waters for us both. A cross-country move eventually teamed me up with David Witkovsky, who brought a whole new approach to my system of alter-identities through his skills in family systems dynamics and conflict resolution while delightfully engaging my intellectual side and teaching me much about the unconscious mind. Another major move led me to Jim Glanzer, who willingly picked up my case and added his gift of spiritual discernment as yet another enhancement to my healing journey.

I'm also extremely grateful for my covenant-keeping husband, who stayed faithfully by my side as we struggled for seven years to figure out what was wrong in my life and who never deserted me after the diagnosis became clear, no matter how rough the emotional roller coaster became. Now God has given us a ministry together, using what we have learned to help others who are experiencing the same type of bondage.

Restoration in Christ Ministries was launched in 1994 as a non-profit organization dedicated to helping survivors of severe, early childhood abuse which has resulted in the development of Dissociative Identity Disorder (DID). We have produced an extensive line of materials, conducted seminars, and done consultations with survivors and their therapists across the country as well as in Canada and Australia.

Of course, my greatest thanks goes to God for preserving my life and my sanity (through the gift of dissociation) as well as my personal relationship to Himself in spite of the evil perpetrated against me. While my faith in His goodness was severely challenged at times, this only made me wrestle harder with Him for answers to my many "Why, God?" questions. As a result I grew immensely in my understanding of Him and the role of Satan and evil in His overall plan for mankind (see Chapter Twelve) and was drawn into an even deeper relationship with Him. I also believe that He is truly taking what Satan intended for evil in my life and using it for good, and I am honored to be His vessel.

Chapter One

Introduction

Formerly called Multiple Personality Disorder, Dissociative Identity Disorder (DID) is a unique psychological condition in which the mind splits itself into multiple identities in order to cope with overwhelming childhood trauma. Amnesic barriers are generally erected between the alter-identities, or "alters," who are formed to enable some parts of the person to be sheltered from the reality of the abuse and thus able to maintain a sense of normalcy in an otherwise intolerable situation. These shielded identities are then able to function in everyday life without being encumbered with the effects of the trauma.

Only a very immature psyche will respond to extreme trauma by creating separate identities. Therefore, DID occurs only in individuals whose trauma *began* before the age of 5 or 6. Once the psyche initiates this type of defense, however, it can continue to create more alter-identities throughout life—whenever it serves a beneficial purpose.

Rather than being a true mental illness, DID actually represents a marvelously creative defense mechanism employed by extremely traumatized children. When they had no way of *external* escape, they found a way to escape the intolerable events *internally*. The condition bears the negative connotation of "disorder" only because its smooth operation often breaks down later in life. Disturbing memories, emotions, and behaviors begin seeping through weakened dissociative barriers, interfering with normal daily living and alerting the unsuspecting Host identity that something is wrong. This is what usually motivates survivors to seek help.

Thankfully, DID is usually treatable in the hands of a knowledgeable therapist and with the proper motivation and cooperation of the survivor. The journey to healing and wholeness is generally an extended and difficult process, however. It requires identifying and resolving the intolerable psychological conflicts which seemingly necessitated the dissociation so that the survivor can own her entire history, including the previously unbearable events. In cases of ritual abuse, varying degrees of mind-control programming and demonization are also involved and further complicate the healing process.

"Ritual abuse" is a term that is sometimes used to refer to any systematic form of abuse inflicted upon another person, usually in a covert manner. This could include any form of repeated, sadistic sexual abuse as well as abuse incurred in conjunction with organized pedophile groups, child pornographers, and child prostitution rings. The underlying motives of these perpetrators are primarily to acquire deviant sexual pleasure and/or financial gain. The damaging effects borne by the children they exploit in these criminal contexts are mammoth. If the victimization began early enough, many of them develop multiple identities in order to cope.

In the field of DID the term "ritual abuse" usually refers to a much more specific type of intense, prolonged, and systematic abuse suffered at the hands of a highly organized perpetrator group devoted to an evil agenda which goes far beyond a purely sadistic or sexual focus. Such groups deliberately inflict severe trauma on young children for the express purpose of inducing dissociation. Once the alter-identities are formed and the amnesic barriers are established to separate them from the primary identities of the person, they then use the alter-identities for mind control experiments, designing them for clandestine purposes serving various schemes obliquely related to national security or world domination.

When such abuse is directly associated with the schemes of devoted Satanists, it is called Satanic Ritual Abuse (SRA). Those familiar with the Bible are quite aware that Satan is actively working through mankind to defeat the Kingdom of God and bring the whole world under his domination. The final outcome of this attempt is vividly described in the biblical book of Revelation. The prolific explosion of SRA survivors emerging around the globe and seeking help is undoubtedly evidence of Satan's advancing endeavors.

While Satan is the mastermind behind all ritual abuse, sometimes the direct connection to him is less clear, as he works under the surface through many types of organizations in different countries of the world. The ostensible goals of these organizations may appear to be religious, civic, or humanitarian in nature, but they usually have a political underpinning. Many are international in scope or moving in that direction. Some even operate under the auspices of government.

The Need for Support

Those whose souls have been literally shattered by extreme trauma, whatever its source or nature, generally need a skilled therapist to address their complex psychological and spiritual needs. Trained clinicians have come to recognize, however, that trauma survivors progress much more quickly when they have some form of support to draw upon outside of their therapy sessions. Many also acknowledge the importance of genuine *love* in the healing process. This is why educating the community at large about the issues and needs of those suffering from DID is so essential.

Almost any multiple (person with DID) will benefit greatly from having a knowledgeable friend who sincerely cares about her with whom she can talk and be "real." If this friend is also willing to pray for her, so much the better.

The degree of support needed beyond this varies greatly among multiples. While some are very capable individuals performing at a professional level, others are quite disabled functionally.

Most lie somewhere between these two extremes. Even those who appear so "together," however, carry tremendous pain, conflict, and turmoil inside. They are just better able to separate, or dissociate, from it in order to function.

The level of neediness and dysfunction within any multiple will also vary along the journey. Don't expect a steady uphill climb marked by consistent improvements. Setbacks can occur at any stage of the process. When therapy gets intense, both emotions and functionality can nose-dive. At other times a single internal victory may produce profound improvement almost overnight.

Marital status is another factor affecting the degree of support a particular multiple needs. In general, those who are living on their own without any kind of healthy support from their families need greater support. If a married survivor's spouse is not handling her diagnosis well or is dysfunctional, abusive, or frequently absent for whatever reason, she too will have increased needs for support. Even having an understanding and supportive spouse does not completely eliminate a survivor's need for additional support, however.

The Benefits of Support

Having a close relationship with another caring individual often provides the sense of safety that is necessary for an abuse survivor to open and face the painful areas of her life that need healing. It also provides an avenue for processing the memories and issues that her various identities bring to the surface, enabling significant therapeutic work to occur between therapy sessions. When the therapist is the only person a survivor can talk to about what is going on in her life, it definitely prolongs the process.

Because many abuse survivors grew up in dysfunctional homes, a supportive relationship can often provide valuable mentoring as well. This may occur naturally as the survivor observes the character qualities and healthy disciplines you have developed. In addition, you may be able to teach her various household or trade skills that you are adept in or avenues of creative expression, such as music, crafts, or other hobbies you enjoy. All of these can be very enriching to a survivor, helping to boost her morale, self-confidence, and productiveness. If you have a strong relationship with God, this too may have a positive impact on her own spirituality.

In the following chapters I will discuss many other more specific types of support that you may be able to offer to those having a history of severe abuse. While not all multiples will need support in all of these areas, they will greatly appreciate having a friend who understands the dynamics described in each chapter.

The Qualities of Supporters

Just as abuse survivors vary in their needs, so do potential support people vary in their ability to minister to those needs. Some individuals are more naturally gifted for this role than others. Some may feel comfortable and capable of giving certain kinds of support but not others. This too is okay. In fact, the most ideal situation is for a survivor to have a *team* of supporters so that the members can complement each other in their roles and no one gets burned out.

If you are dealing with heavy issues of your own, you may not have the emotional capacity to become deeply involved with a multiple, or you may have to limit yourself to specific types of support that require little emotional involvement. You should also be aware that supporting a multiple through *her* abuse issues may bring buried wounds and unresolved issues of *your own* to the surface. If this occurs, remember that taking care of yourself is equally as important as ministering to the survivor's needs. Do not try to be a super-hero or a martyr. Thank God for using this situation to bring to your attention these areas in your own life that need to be addressed, and take the time to do so. I truly believe that most survivors will understand this.

The availability of time is another variable in the lives of potential support people that must be considered. Once a caring relationship is established, some particularly "needy" survivors can be quite demanding of your time. Therefore, if you do commit yourself to supporting a survivor, you must be able to set firm boundaries so that your own needs, the needs of your family, and your other responsibilities will not be neglected. Doing this will model proper self-care to the survivor, who often needs to grow in this area too. For this reason people with co-dependent tendencies do not make good support people no matter how much time they have available.

At the very least a support person needs to be comfortable with emotions and abuse issues and understand the basic dynamics of DID and ritual abuse (if necessary). This can be acquired by reading materials and attending seminars on the subject as well as by consulting with others more familiar with the diagnosis. You can also learn a lot from the survivor herself as you proceed in the relationship. Many are very willing to help others grow in understanding if it will provide greater support for themselves.

Good interpersonal skills are also important. These include respect, compassion, and sensitivity as well as the ability to be a good listener and to maintain objectivity. Living a healthy and moral lifestyle is also beneficial since you are apt to become a role model for the survivor.

I believe spiritual health is just as important. You will have so much more to offer a survivor if you have a strong relationship with God and a vital prayer life so that you can draw upon His strength, wisdom, and grace in the many challenges you will undoubtedly encounter. A strong faith in God and His character will also provide stability as you grapple with the existence of evil of unimaginable proportions. In addition, having a firm grasp of spiritual warfare principles will prepare you to respond effectively should you encounter demonic forces associated with SRA survivors.

Even with all this, however, you still need a willingness to learn and grow and be stretched in what will be a very unique type of relationship. Remember, however, that whatever God requires of you will be matched by His all-sufficient supply of grace, strength, wisdom, and love!

The Rewards of Supporters

If you do decide to enter into a support relationship with a multiple, in whatever capacity, God will not leave you unrewarded. You may find the relationship very enriching to yourself as well, as many multiples are extremely talented and gifted individuals who make wonderful friends. Many also have great spiritual depth.

God will undoubtedly use the challenges you face within the relationship to mature and refine your character for His glory. I believe He will also lead you to a deeper understanding of Himself, Satan, and the spiritual realm.

You will also share in the thrill of watching the survivor receive deep inner healing and be restored to the wholeness God intended for her. If you are supporting a ritual abuse survivor, you will additionally witness the power of God triumphing over evil and releasing the survivor from bondage to the powers of darkness. This joy will be beyond compare—to say nothing of the reward awaiting you in heaven from Jesus Himself (Mark 9:41; Matthew 25:34-40).

Chapter Two

Building Trust

Trust is the foundational cornerstone of any significant relationship. Trust doesn't come easily, however, if you were repeatedly hurt by those you trusted as a child. Therefore, developing any kind of close relationship with another person can be scary for an abuse survivor. Many find themselves caught in a conflict in which they long to have a supportive, caring relationship but at the same time are very frightened by that prospect.

As a potential supporter, you need to understand this fear and recognize that learning to trust again may come slowly for a survivor. Therefore, do not push yourself too aggressively into a relationship with one. No matter how good your intentions may be, this will usually heighten her fears and defenses. Instead, be gentle, patient, and sensitive to how far she opens the door to you.

Learning to trust again is a critical component of the healing process, however. A survivor obviously has to trust a therapist in order to reveal the deepest parts of her soul where truth and healing is most needed. Hopefully she will also be willing to trust others, especially those whom God may graciously send to walk alongside her on what will be a very challenging journey.

Like most people, the way survivors evaluate trustworthiness is greatly affected by their personal history. Their abuse not only tinted the glasses through which they view people but usually resulted in the development of incredible "radar" for reading people. Therefore, you may find yourself being scrutinized as never before.

Their carefully attuned antennae will be particularly sensitive to anything that likens you to their perpetrators, whether the similarities are physical attributes, particular mannerisms, or character traits. Obviously, some of these things are totally irrational indicators of danger, but they will nevertheless sound an internal alarm and evoke a cautious response in survivors.

They may eventually be able to overcome their unfounded fears based on superficial resemblances but will need your patience and understanding in the process. Character issues are of much greater importance, however, because of how severely they were impacted by their absence in their perpetrator(s). If unresolved, they can be fatal to the relationship.

Because abuse survivors were deliberately lied to so many times and experienced so many broken promises, they usually carry a deeply rooted belief that actions are a much more reliable indicator of reality than words. Therefore, in the early stages of your relationship the survivor is apt to note very carefully how well your actions match the words you speak. Only when she is convinced of their consistency will she begin trusting your words alone.

Furthermore, most abuse survivors know all too well that "bad guys" can dress well, talk smoothly, and give out candy. Therefore, they will generally not put much stock on superficialities but will instead cautiously wait to see how your true inner character reveals itself.

Heading the list of character traits that will help to win the trust of abuse survivors is **moral integrity** with its many corollaries. This was totally absent or utterly inconsistent in their abusers. In fact, some may not even know what true moral integrity looks like in a person. They do know, however, how greatly they were hurt by people who constantly deceived them and had no regard for any standard of human decency and respect. Therefore, they have virtually no tolerance for any kind of duplicity, deception, or disregard for their personhood.

For them, a trustworthy relationship must be marked by absolute **honesty** as well as **respect** and **kindness**. Because many have never experienced it, being treated with respect, and even dignity, is often an awesome "door opener" for trust and a new kind of relationship.

Consistency is also of heightened importance because of how inconsistently their abusers treated them. Just as your words and actions must match, so must the way you treat them from day to day. Therefore, if you decide to change the dynamics of the relationship, be sure to inform them of this as well as your reasons for the change.

Dependability is equally important. This means following through with whatever plans or promises you make—or carefully explaining why you couldn't. Unexpected changes are particularly unsettling because of how often this has previously heralded the onset of abuse for them.

Openness is another crucial quality. They have too often been deeply hurt by the sly and covert manipulations and deceptions of their perpetrators. Therefore, if they detect anything going on behind their backs, it can strike terror in their hearts! Some may even find it difficult to trust that a secret can ever be meant for their good. They may have to learn what you mean by a "good secret."

Firm moral and personal boundaries are extremely important for two reasons. First of all, because they have had their boundaries violated so much in the past, survivors are usually supersensitive to any inappropriate or uninvited intrusion into their "personal space." People who try to come too close too soon make them uncomfortable. On the other hand, they need *others* to have firm boundaries because sometimes they have no idea where boundaries should be placed. So they often find themselves over-reacting in opposite directions regarding boundaries—but that kind of inconsistency is what DID is all about!

A quality which really impresses survivors is a willingness to **acknowledge mistakes.** While they generally want you to be perfect—at the other end of the performance spectrum from their abusers—to a certain extent they realize that you can't be. So acknowledging when you "goof" will go a long way in redeeming yourself in their eyes. None of their abusers ever did that!

Sensitivity is also important. Although their abuse often hardened them to endure extraordinary physical adversity, it has left most survivors supersensitive emotionally. Any perceived hint of mistreatment can tap into deep, unhealed wounds and evoke a major reaction emotionally. In such a case protector alters may even emerge to defend them or to retaliate in an aggressive manner. Sensitivity is needed not only to avoid setting off such a reaction but also to handle the situation when it occurs.

Furthermore, because of their traumatic childhoods, survivors invariably have many alter-identities with distorted and negative views of life and people. You will need particular sensitivity to relate to them in a validating manner that doesn't reinforce their negative perceptions but instead opens the door to constructive dialogue.

Torturous abuse also leaves its victims with a host of irrational fears and peculiar reactions to seemingly innocuous things. Some of these were deliberately programmed into them while others are a natural aftermath of the terrifying things to which they were subjected. While you cannot possibly be sensitive to all of their "triggers" before you know them, your handling them delicately when you *do* become aware of them means a lot. Through genuine understanding and support you may even be able to assist them in gaining victory over these troublesome reactions.

Developing sensitivity in all of these areas will take time. You may learn by mistakes, but if you can maintain a teachable spirit at those times and discuss with the survivor what went wrong, the relationship will probably not be damaged.

Compassion is another critical attribute for a support person. While survivors may recognize your legitimate need to set boundaries on the extent of your emotional involvement with them, they need to feel that you are genuinely moved by the horrific abuse they have suffered, even if you choose not to know the details of it. If you maintain too cold or aloof an attitude, you will rarely get in the front door with them. They will be too apt to read your extreme emotional detachment as disbelief or judgment.

Your **non-judgmental acceptance of all their alters** is also important. Although as a support person you will not necessarily meet every one of them, you never know who may emerge in a given situation. They are not all naturally amicable or endowed with social graces. While some are happy, carefree, and delightful, others may be angry, vulgar, aggressive, seductive, or deeply withdrawn. You may be surprised to meet alters of both sexes as well as a wide span of ages. All of this may be difficult to comprehend initially, but hopefully you will quickly adjust and be able to welcome and relate equally well to whomever appears.

Accepting each of a survivor's alters is vital for several reasons. First of all, distinguishing alters as "good" or "bad" enhances internal conflict and perpetuates the need for their ongoing separation (see Chapter Four). Secondly, judgment or rejection closes the door of opportunity for influencing change in their perspectives and behaviors. Finally, by readily accepting all of their alters, you become a powerful model to them. If they are ever to reunite with all of them, the process begins with acceptance—and sometimes that's hard for them too.

Closely related to acceptance is having **respect for each alter's contribution**. Always remember that whatever characteristics are manifested on the surface, every alter serves a protective purpose. When you probe into the history of the most obnoxious or antagonistic alters, you will learn the crucial role they played in taking on what was perceived to be intolerable in order to spare the Core. Keeping this in mind will greatly enhance your appreciation and respect for them.

While demonstrating these qualities will usually provide a solid foundation for a survivor's trust, in some cases the fear of trust may be so strong that she is unable to overcome it, no matter how trustworthy you prove yourself to be. In these instances she may need gentle assistance in identifying and challenging the beliefs underlying her fears.

Your opportunity to play a role in this may be limited, but perhaps through a letter you could make a final attempt to prod her thinking in a productive direction. Try to help her see that although her fear is legitimate and understandable in light of her personal history, it is depriving her of desirable benefits now. Just because she was consistently hurt as a child by those she tried to trust, this is not true *all* the time with *all* people. You might try pointing out others who seemingly enjoy relationships of trust without getting hurt. Challenge her to move from applying her fear of trust globally to *all* people in *all* situations to learning how to assess which people are trustworthy and which are not.

Sometimes the survivor may have to process some of her memories of when her trust was painfully betrayed and get healing for those wounds before trust will be able to grow again. Therefore, encourage her to discuss her fear of trust with her therapist.

Whatever the situation, don't ever force yourself into a relationship with a survivor. Respect her viewpoint if she, for some reason, does not feel comfortable or safe in pursuing it. Having a *choice* is a precious, and often new, realization for a survivor, and learning to utilize it is often a major step in the healing process too.

Even when a survivor responds positively to you, proceed slowly and cautiously. Recognize that this relationship will be much more complex than any you have previously experienced. Because of this, both survivor and support person do well to wade into it gradually.

Chapter Three

Understanding Dissociation

In its simplest form dissociation is something that most people experience in their daily lives. The most common example is day-dreaming, which occurs when your mind becomes so absorbed in thought or fanciful imagination that it completely loses touch with your physical surroundings. When you "wake up" from this experience, you remember nothing of what occurred while you were so deeply engrossed mentally. If this occurs while you are driving, it is called "highway hypnosis," and in this case your body carried out some very critical actions without the conscious direction of your mind.

This normal kind of dissociation can occur *only* when the activity being carried out by the body is so familiar that the brain has literally programmed itself to carry it out automatically without the direction of the mind. The consequences of normal dissociation are very slight because the instant the brain encounters something that is out of the ordinary, it summons the attention of the mind, which brings the person back in touch with his external environment. For instance, if you are engrossed in "highway hypnosis" and suddenly encounter an animal on the road, your brain will instantly draw your wandering mind back to your driving so that you can maneuver around it.

Dissociative Identity Disorder

The phenomenon of dissociation lies on a continuum, however, that progresses to conditions which become increasingly more pathological and disruptive to normal functioning. Dissociative Identity Disorder is the most extreme form, involving the complete splitting of the soul. Since the soul encompasses the mind, will, and emotions of the person, each split-off part will have its own independently functioning mind, will, and emotions.

This most extreme form of dissociation is initiated when an immature child experiences a distressing event of unbearable magnitude. She is powerless to escape physically; nor can she use normal dissociation to disengage her mind in its entirety from her external environment—because her brain has not been programmed to handle the event without the involvement of her mind.

At this intolerable and inescapable moment of time, the child's totally overwhelmed amygdala (organ in the brain) is able to shut down her normal consciousness in the front of the brain,[1] where her Core Self is centered, and shift it to the back of her brain. Here she forms a sequestered pocket of consciousness that endures the intolerable trauma in the external environment. If intolerable trauma continues to occur in the child's life, many such "pockets" may be formed and gradually develop into distinct alter-identities having their own independent minds, wills, and emotions.

Because traumatic events are just as overwhelming to these "victim alters," they will often utilize some other adaptive coping strategy to lessen the full impact of the event. The creativity they exhibit in doing so is often amazing.

Some may use a further "partial dissociation," shutting down conscious awareness of one or more, but not all, of the physical senses. One may determine, for instance "I am going to *see* this but not *feel* it," and somehow dissociate her sense of touch away from her conscious awareness.

If she cannot totally dissociate her sense of touch, she may use imagination to lessen the degree to which she experiences it. For instance, she may imagine that she has skin like an alligator and do this so successfully that her sensations of touch and pain are truly diminished.

Another alternative is for an alter-identity to use imagination to decrease her sense of connection to her body. She may, for instance, perceive herself to be floating above her body, watching the traumatic event transpire below, or she may imagine that she exists only in her head, not in her body.

Victim alters can also lessen the impact of traumatic events through various avenues of reinterpretation. They may reinterpret the meaning of the event to eliminate the intolerable element. For instance, a child alter who is being molested may tell herself, "This is what Daddy does to show me how much he loves me."

Reinterpretation can be used rather freely to change aspects of the alter's identity, or perception of self. This may involve changing her body image to make her feel stronger or more powerful. She may, for instance, perceive herself as having a body that is more husky or older than it really is.

Reinterpreting one's identity may even involve gender if it will in some way provide an increased sense of safety, worth, strength, or morality. Reinterpretation of sexual orientation is also possible. When this occurs, it has a very distinct purpose and may actually enable the alter to preserve a sense of morality, as illustrated below.

When a victim alter cannot avoid participating in immoral activities, she may redefine her moral standards, perhaps devising a way to justify the activities of her perpetrators. This is often the only way she can lessen the intolerable level of guilt she would otherwise feel.

Sometimes the victim alter left to handle the traumatic event will opt out of the unbearable situation altogether. In this case a switch will occur to send out another alter or a new one will be created to handle the situation.

When under extreme duress, the mind is so incredibly masterful in doing whatever is necessary to lessen the intolerable nature of an event. Not only can it create separate identities in one person, but it can also design each one to fit the exact need of the moment.

Consider, for instance, the case of a dissociative young teen who is forced into prostitution by her perpetrator. When she is handed over to a man at a luxury hotel, "Georgia" is designated to be "out" to fulfill the role. She is able to do so by reinterpreting the meaning of the event as an opportunity to receive affection and affirmation as a female. This works fine until her clothes start coming off and the time for the sex act arrives. At that point she can no longer cope with the situation and totally escapes, sending out "Sylvia" to take her place.

This sensitive young alter is absolutely horrified to find herself naked in bed with a strange man. Whatever her particular "piece" of life history has been, she firmly believes that nudity is absolutely forbidden between the sexes. The situation is so intolerable to her that she quickly escapes back inside as well.

Since part of the person *has* to go through with the immoral sex act, the person creates a totally new alter. This alter reinterprets her identity to be not only male—but a homosexual male. This enables "him" to tolerate what is now perceived as "same sex nudity." He is also able to go through the required sex act by reinterpreting its meaning to be a "celebration of the male body." How this is perceived to work out anatomically defies rational thought but is seemingly no problem for a "redesigned" and dissociated alter.

The Nature of Alter-Identities

Because of the amnesic barriers existing between the alters, they each carry a different set of memories. In a very real sense each one has her own unique life history, however long or short it might be. Each one is also shaped by the specific set of memories she carries.

Since memory plays a significant role in the learning process, a survivor's alters may not all know how to do the same things. For instance, "Mary" may know how to balance a checkbook, but "Jane" does not. "Jane," however, may know how to cook while "Mary" doesn't.

Memory also affects one's interpretation of situations. Therefore, "Susie" may equate closed doors with a need for privacy while "Mary" equates them with anger, rejection, and abandonment.

Emotional responses are also integrally connected to memory. Therefore, "Karen," who has been internally sheltered from the abuse, may run fearlessly to Daddy while "Judy" trembles with fear when he enters a room.

Different life experiences also lead to different conclusions about, and patterns of relating to, self, others, and the environment, which means that the different identities will have different personalities. This is what made the former label of Multiple Personality Disorder so appropriate!

In actual fact, however, most of the split-off parts will not accumulate a sufficient life history of their own to develop a fully rounded personality. They still have a distinct, dissociated identity, however, which makes the current label of Dissociative Identity Disorder perhaps more accurate.

The Operational Dynamics of the Alter-Identities

Obviously when multiple identities are formed within a single person, they must be organized in some way so the individual has a sense of order and stability in her life rather than one big "free-for-all" amongst the various identities. Therefore, the same ingenuity that uniquely designs each alter also creates an organizational structure to keep track of them all and to define their operational dynamics. This plan generally establishes an authority structure as well as a prescribed way for the alters to move in and out of consciousness and participation in external life. This plan is usually depicted internally through mental imagery, although the Host may not be consciously aware of it.

Alter-identities are usually created to serve distinct functions within the system and will be arranged accordingly. Many exist solely to embody trauma. These are called "victim alters," and they will generally only participate in life during traumatic events or when something in the immediate environment reminds them of their trauma. In this latter situation the emerging alter is said to have been "triggered."

Other alters may serve as "protectors." They usually take on a rather tough façade and often carry a lot of anger. They are designed to protect the individual or particular identities from any perceived danger or further abuse. While their effectiveness in standing up against a perpetrator was limited, they often intervened to take abuse in the place of weaker alters. They can be quite aggressive in attempting to fulfill their protective role with any other perceived threat in the survivor's life, however.

"Controller alters" are the designated leaders in the system. They have the highest authority and decide who participates in life at any given time. They usually operate behind the scenes and rarely participate in external life themselves. They are obviously key identities with whom to establish trust and cooperation.

"Caretakers" are usually older alters who care for very young alters internally. They may speak for these alters as well, which is helpful in therapy.

"Function alters" are designed to carry out specific functions in the person's life, usually unrelated to trauma. They may perform certain chores or participate in specific activities. They may pursue special interests, hobbies, or the development of a unique talent.

"Presenters" are the identities who handle normal, daily living. Collectively this group of identities are called the "Presenter System." They are the alters who predominantly interact with life in non-abusive settings and are most known by other people.

The "Host" is the strongest of the Presenters and the one who handles life most frequently. The Host is usually closely related to the Core Self. (See Appendix B for a complete list of the various types of alters.)

The alter-identities within each individual will usually exhibit a distinct pattern by which they "present" or interact with the external world. In the stereotypical cases presented in the well-known movies "The Three Faces of Eve" and "Sybil," only one alter participated in life at a time, and the other alters were usually totally amnesic for the time periods in which another alter was "out." These blackout periods are referred to as "lost time." This type of presentation produces significant gaps in memory for virtually all the identities.

In other cases, the entire Presenter System shares a co-consciousness, but only one of these identities is actually in control of the body at a time. In this more common situation "lost time" generally occurs only when an identity who is not part of the Presenter System comes out to fulfill a particular purpose, such as handling abusive episodes in the person's life. Sometimes the Presenter System will remain co-conscious when some of these other alters come out as well. This varies greatly among multiples and generally increases as they move toward healing.

For some individuals, the entire Presenter System is involved in living life all at the same time. In this situation the person may express markedly different perspectives within the same conversation. This individual often appears flighty in both her thoughts and actions, which rapidly send her in different directions. This is an extremely difficult kind of system to recognize and interact with knowledgeably.

Another subtle type of Presenter System occurs when the Host personality serves as a "Shell." In this case the Host is like a glove into which the various other alters come to present. The Shell consistently functions as the speaker but will reflect the personality, emotions, and perspectives of the particular alter who is "filling" her. This "hand-in-glove" type of presentation enables the person to maintain a sense of consistent identity externally as well as a continuous short-term memory. It also minimizes the appearance of switching between the various alters.

Alters existing outside of the Presenter System are sometimes arranged in layers or different sub-systems, which may be managed separately. These alters will vary considerably in the degree of awareness they have of each other and external life.

Endnote

[1]James Wilder, Thrive Conference, Baldwin, Michigan, October 2002.

Chapter Four

Memory

Memory is obviously a key focus in bringing healing to trauma survivors. In many cases, however, distinct memories of the trauma are either unavailable or not readily accessible. This is particularly true if the traumatic events took place during the first few years of life or were so intolerable that the memories were dissociated out of the normal stream of consciousness.[1]

Some of these dissociated memories may be retrieved, but a major debate exists over how reliable "recovered memories" are. At one extreme are certain clinicians who, in the past at least, believed that every image that came into a survivor's head was a precisely recorded memory. At the other extreme are certain groups who try very hard to sway the media and convince the world that "recovered memories" simply do not exist. Unfortunately, the general public is not informed enough about the dynamics of memory to be able to evaluate this issue from an educated perspective.

Because the perceived need for denial is one of the most powerful dynamics seemingly necessitating dissociation, survivors themselves also get caught up in the debate over what is true and what is not. Most would love to believe that the memories returning to them are not true, and yet something has to explain all the other symptoms occurring in their lives. Furthermore, research has definitely concluded that a diagnosis of DID presupposes a history of extreme early childhood trauma.[2] Discerning the exact nature of that trauma is not always easy, however.

Cases do exist in which a person's so-called "recovered memories" do not reflect reality. Certain individuals may observe and savor the secondary gain that can be reaped from being an "abuse victim" to the extent that their minds produce imaginary images reported as "recovered memories." Perhaps someone has suggested to them that their symptoms might be rooted in trauma or abuse that they do not remember. This, unfortunately, can be a great springboard for an imaginative mind to become activated in fulfilling this expectation.

Other individuals may possess extremely fanciful and dissociative minds, losing themselves so completely in books they read or movies they watch that they are eventually unable to separate what they truly experienced from that which they absorbed so deeply through an artificial means. In time, the incongruities of their reported images and their other symptomatology, or lack thereof, may distinguish these persons from true abuse survivors.[3]

While these examples probably represent extreme possibilities, the confirmed suggestibility of the mind is a complicating factor that cannot be ignored in evaluating "recovered memories." It is much more apt to play a role in the lives of true abuse survivors who are trying to understand more fully just what happened to them. Perhaps the memories emerging from their minds have revealed just scanty bits and pieces of trauma that do not give a complete picture, or their trauma occurred at a pre-verbal age and is evident only from their diagnosis or symptomatology. In these cases the mind's natural bent towards "making sense" out of life[4] leaves it prone to suggestibility and imagination.[5]

Because memory is such a critical, but often ambiguous, issue in DID, becoming more knowledgeable of this subject is extremely important for both survivors and those working with them. Drawing upon the early observations of Pierre Janet as well as current research, Dr. Bessel van der Kolk and his colleagues have contributed much in the way of helping us gain greater insight into how our bodies record the events that happen to us, how these memories get "played back" to us, and to what degree we can trust their accuracy. Dr. van der Kolk is a research psychiatrist at Boston University, who is viewed as an expert in the field of trauma.

Narrative Memory

Memory is not a simple subject to study. It gets stored in different ways and in different places within our bodies. The type of memory scientists know most about is what they call "Narrative Memory." This corresponds to what most people think of when using the term "memory." Technically, this is memory that is put into language and made part of one's total life experience.[6]

Narrative Memory is stored in the hippocampus, a deep inner organ of the brain that is not completely developed until the third to fifth year of life. The process by which Narrative Memory is collected and recorded begins with data being picked up from the environment by the sensory organs. This data travels along neural pathways to specific sensory receptor sites in the brain. From there the data is brought together and loosely assembled into a unit by the thalamus. It then goes to the amygdala, which emotionally assesses it. The amygdala's response determines how extensively and accurately the data will be recorded by the hippocampus.[7]

When spurred into action by the amygdala, the hippocampus translates the data into narrative form (words), organizes, indexes, and stores it. All of this occurs on an unconscious level. Only the data that is processed and stored in the hippocampus gets sent on to the pre-frontal cortex where it can be further evaluated and utilized by the individual on a conscious level. This is also the only data that the individual can voluntarily recall as "memory."[8]

Because the interaction between the amygdala and hippocampus is critical in determining what we can consciously remember, it deserves further explanation. To do so, I would like to put van der Kolk's hypothesis concerning these dynamics into an analogy. Let's consider "Hippo" to be the librarian of a massive internal library. Hippo's job is to take the data that is brought to him and to sort it into books of various titles. All through our lives he continues to sort incoming data into these books, creating new books as necessary and constantly adding to and modifying the existing books.[9]

Hippo cannot record *all* the data picked up by our sensory organs. Therefore, he has "Amy Amygdala" posted in front of his office. Amy is a very emotional female who immediately reacts to the incoming data. Hippo watches her through the window in his office to see how excited she becomes in response to the data. The more she reacts, the more he records.

If Amy considers the data coming in to be familiar and expected,[10] she shows little reaction to it, so Hippo pays little attention and records very little of the data.[11] In essence Amy serves to filter out all the ordinary, mundane, and unimportant data from a given experience. This explains why most people do not remember all the cars, houses, or people they pass on their way to work, for instance. This is considered unessential information by Amy.

If, however, the data seems to be important or interesting to Amy, she becomes somewhat more aroused. This signals Hippo to pay attention and record the data.[12] Encountering a Rolls Royce on the way to work, for instance, is much more likely to be remembered because of its unusual nature. If this is not the first time that the individual has encountered a Rolls Royce, Hippo will quickly open his already established book entitled "Cars" to the chapter devoted to Rolls Royces. He will then focus his attention on what parts of the current experience serve to broaden or modify the data already stored in this file and will record this with considerable accuracy.[13]

However, if the data which Amy considers interesting or important is so new that Hippo has no suitable "book" already created in which to store the information, his focus will be primarily upon making a new book and determining a "title" to put on it. This will decrease both the amount and the degree of detail he is able to record on this new subject. What he does record will also be more prone to inaccuracies.[14] This means that when you come out of a lecture on a brand new subject, you will remember much less of it than a person who is already well acquainted with the subject.

Encountering a situation which is strikingly unusual, unexpected, or frightening[15] will cause Amy to become intensely aroused. Hippo will thus be alerted to pay extreme attention and record the data with great accuracy.[16] This is why certain outstanding experiences, such as viewing the Grand Canyon or Niagara Falls for the first time, may be indelibly impressed in one's memory.

Many traumatic experiences have the same effect. In these cases, because the sensory data was received and processed by Hippo, the memories can be willfully and consciously recalled. Because they were recorded under conditions of heightened emotional arousal in Amy and with Hippo at full attention, they will also be remembered in abnormally vivid and complete detail. This is referred to as "hypermnesia" (the opposite of amnesia) and is typical of isolated traumatic incidents occurring to older children and adults.[17] These memories are highly resistant to distortion over time.[18]

Traumatic Memory

When a traumatic experience creates an *intolerable* level of psychic distress, Amy's *excessive* emotional arousal seemingly impairs the neurological pathway to Hippo.[19] In this case *he receives no data from the event at all.* This means there is no narrative record of it. It does not enter into the individual's recorded "biography of life,"[20] nor can it be voluntarily recalled.[21] As a result, the individual experiences what van der Kolk calls "chronic dissociative amnesia," having no conscious memory of the event. This, he says, is more typical in cases of repeated, severe traumatization occurring in early childhood.[22]

The rerouted data from these terrifying events remains unprocessed and is stored outside of the hippocampus as emotionally charged sensory imprints.[23] These individual, isolated memory pockets are so different from Narrative Memory that they belong in a separate classification known as "Traumatic Memory."[24]

Unlike Narrative Memory, Traumatic Memory can only be recalled if the person happens to be in a situation that is in some way reminiscent of the original terrifying event.[25] Encountering a distinct reminder of the trauma seems to provide a neural connection which allows the memory, or parts of it, to surface into consciousness.

Because the data was only minimally processed from its raw sensory form, the memory, when triggered, will be experienced as a virtual replay of the physical sensations, and often the emotions, which occurred in the original event.[26] While the various sensory aspects of the memory may not surface all at once,[27] the person will once again see, hear, smell, taste, and feel the physical sensations of the trauma as if it were recurring in the present.[28] In psychological terms this re-experience of a traumatic event is called an "abreaction."

The Accuracy of Traumatic Memory Versus Narrative Memory

One cannot apply studies regarding the accuracy of Narrative Memory to Traumatic Memory, as some would advocate. Because they are routed and stored so differently, the reliability of each must be considered separately. Failure to recognize this is one of the key fallibilities of those who contest the veracity of recovered traumatic memories.

The accuracy of Narrative Memory is determined by the quality of the original record and the degree of distortion which takes place after it is recorded. Initially, the extent and accuracy of the original record depends upon the familiarity of the event, the emotional assessment of it, and the degree of mental attention paid to it, as described above.

After an event is recorded as Narrative Memory, distortion can occur in at least two manners. First of all, distortion can occur within the hippocampus as new data is combined with previously recorded, similar data.[29] Way back in 1889, Pierre Janet recognized that "once a particular event or bit of information becomes integrated in a larger scheme, it will no longer be accessible as an individual entity, and hence the memory will be distorted."[30]

The second factor that can cause distortion in Narrative Memory is the social modification that takes place and gets re-enforced in recounting it to others.[31] For instance, how you describe an event to your husband may be somewhat different from how you describe it to your mother, depending on the effect you want it to have. You may want your husband to be extremely concerned while not wanting to unduly alarm your mother. Obviously, the possibility of social distortion increases the more an event is recounted to others.

The accuracy of Traumatic Memory is extremely different. Janet described Traumatic Memory as "inflexible and invariable."[32] Because these memories are stored as isolated imprints in the brain, the original record is not distorted by any subsequent data being added to it.[33] Furthermore, these memories have been stored outside the normal stream of consciousness. Therefore, they have not been subjected to distortion through social interactions either.[34]

The extreme accuracy of Traumatic Memory applies only to the original, sensory re-experience of the event, however. Once it has been evoked into consciousness, the memory of its recall becomes a Narrative Memory stored in the hippocampus. This "memory of remembering" is then subject to the distortion possibilities inherent to all Narrative Memory.[35]

Furthermore, van der Kolk's reference to the sensory "imprints" of Traumatic Memory would seemingly imply that the event was recorded in "snapshot" form rather than as a complete "video." In fact, the process of retrieving all of the sensory imprints from a single event may extend over a period of time.[36] Because the mind uses memory to try to make sense out of life,[37] errors could occur in the way that it interprets the pieces that are recalled or in the way that it tries to fill in the gaps between the pieces.[38] Imagination and suggestibility can play a significant role in this process.

Survivors can subconsciously glean suggestions from the questions, cues, or expectations of other people or from other sources of information to which they have been exposed, such as books, lectures, TV programs, movies, etc. For this reason those working with abuse survivors must be extremely careful in their interactions with them. Conveying pre-conceived ideas or hunches about what you think may have happened in their lives or asking leading or presumptive questions of them can significantly impact their minds. In the long run it may also increase the struggles they have over whether their memories came from your suggestions or from reality inside themselves. Allowing specific information regarding the nature of the trauma a survivor has suffered to come out of her own recollection is always best.

Because of the natural inclination that survivors usually have to seek out any possible resource to help them understand what they are experiencing, keeping their minds totally devoid of influence by suggestion is probably impossible. In all likelihood most survivors will have at least a scattered sprinkling of suggestion-derived material throughout the composite picture they will each eventually construct of their personal history. This degree of contamination may be inconsequential. However, when major pieces of the puzzle come from suggestion, that can be problematic. Among other things, it can misguide the course of therapy away from the true issues needing healing.

The identification of perpetrators is certainly a major and very critical piece of the memory picture, and it is not immune from suggestion. For this reason accusation of perpetrators based solely on "recovered memories" is not advised. Such information should be held in abeyance until stronger evidence emerges either to confirm or to exonerate supposed perpetrators.

Implicit Memory

The way that the body records the events that occur to it is actually much broader than what we now know as Narrative and Traumatic Memory, and the organs involved extend far beyond the brain. Another manner in which traumatic events leave imprints on a person is through what is known as "Implicit Memory." This refers to the ongoing effects of an event that are demonstrated in a person's life even when no cognitive memory exists of what caused them. In other words, just as you can tell an abused dog from a well-cared-for dog by the way it acts, [39] traumatized people live out the effects of their abuse in many non-verbal ways.[40]

The ongoing effects of trauma can encompass a person's perception, emotions, behavior, body functions, and sleep patterns. In most cases, however, the individual has no idea *why* he reacts the way he does, *why* some of the physical systems of his body are malfunctioning, or *why* he struggles with insomnia or nightmares.

Whatever the symptoms are, they are all evidence of Implicit Memory, and they can often provide significant pieces of data in deciphering what has happened to an individual. Sometimes Implicit Memory serves as the *only* indicator that a person has suffered some kind of significant trauma.[41] This is especially true if the event(s) occurred in the early childhood years. In the absence of cognitive memory, these symptoms sometimes speak louder than words.

In cases in which Traumatic Memories *are* being recovered, Implicit Memory can sometimes play an important role in validating them. For instance, if I have had an unusual, lifelong fear of birds and then one day recover a Traumatic Memory of being locked in a small cage with several large black birds, my lifelong fear of birds—which is the Implicit Memory—validates the recovered Traumatic Memory.

Because severe, childhood trauma *always* leaves telltale indicators in a person's life, one does not have to rely entirely on one type of memory to determine that it really happened. Understanding the entire memory picture is imperative, especially when evaluating the controversial recovered memory issue. *True Traumatic Memory never arises in a vacuum with no other signs of abuse.*

Body Memory

Another form of memory is tied very specifically to the physical body. While Body Memory symptoms have long been observed in connection with trauma survivors,[42] only recently have scientists discovered that virtually every cell of the body carries a capacity for memory. This is being strikingly demonstrated in transplant recipients—who often start manifesting characteristics of the donor or having nightmares about something that happened in the donor's life.

Most typically, Body Memory refers to physical injuries reminiscent of a past trauma that reappear on a person's body when the memory surfaces or the person encounters a powerful reminder of it.[43] At these times welts, bruises, abrasions, or burns may become transiently visible on the body.

Body Memory can also refer to the physical pressure or pain felt during abreactions. As explained above, true Traumatic Memories are generally recalled as a replay of the sensory data from the original event. This includes the sensations of touch and pain, which are felt in the exact place(s) on or in the body as occurred during the actual event.

Psychosomatic symptoms may technically be a form of Implicit Memory, but they are reflected in the body. Like other Body Memories, they are directly related to a specific unresolved past trauma[44] but are more chronic in nature. They usually involve ongoing, though sometimes intermittent, pain in a particular part of the body or a persistent malfunction in one of the body systems for which no physical cause can be found.

Because of this phenomenon, abuse survivors tend to make frequent trips to the doctor or emergency room—only to be told that the doctor can find nothing wrong. This is not only embarrassing to the survivor, but it can also leave her confused about when she should consider her symptoms a significant current problem that needs to be addressed.

Another form of Body Memory involves an unnatural physical response in the body that occurs when a reminder of a previous trauma is encountered. Something that is seen, heard, read, or recalled spontaneously evokes a physical jolt, a deep sinking feeling in the chest or stomach, sudden anxiety or panic, or practically any unnatural expression of fright.[45] For instance, if you encounter an article on child pornography in a magazine and suddenly have a deep, sinking feeling in your stomach and an accelerated heart rate, your body is remembering something it has personally experienced in connection with this subject. It is shouting a message to you!

The body is definitely involved in "remembering" trauma events. As van der Kolk says, "The body keeps score!"[46] even when other forms of memory are scant. He also claims that while the mind is suggestible—the body is not! Body Memories, therefore, are extremely valid indicators of abuse. When they occur as a Traumatic Memory is being recalled, they provide extremely significant confirmation of the memory!

Early Memory

Typically, memories of one's first few years of life are scarce. This is because the myelination of the hippocampus is not complete until age three to five.[47] In other words, "Hippo's library" is still under construction. Without a functioning hippocampus, Narrative memory is impossible. Therefore, early memory is limited to non-verbal forms, including Traumatic Memory, Implicit Memory, and Body Memory.

Some form of memory, possibly connected with the person's immaterial soul or spirit, even seems to occur within the womb. Evidence certainly indicates that a child's learning process begins during a pre-birth stage of development. An unborn baby can learn to recognize voices and even to learn music scores.[48] Infants can also act out trauma occurring in the birth process, such as having the umbilical cord wrapped around its neck[49] or having its mouth forcefully suctioned out.[50]

Although more difficult to substantiate, Implicit Memory effects can possibly be traced back to intra-uterine experiences as well. The above examples certainly indicate that a developing fetus at some stage acquires an awareness of, and even an attentiveness to, sound outside the womb. Whether that sound is frequently loud, hostile, and raucous or predominately calm and nurturing is likely to have an impact on the baby both before and after birth.

Some counselors have observed a *possible* correlation between specific issues some individuals struggle with and the attitude of their mothers towards them while they were in the womb.[51] This might indicate a degree of sensitivity between the child's spirit and the mother's spirit, allowing the child to pick up such things as a mother's displeasure toward the pregnancy, her consideration of abortion, or her strong desire for a child of a certain sex. While this is perhaps speculative, it deserves mention.

Apart from what may, or may not, occur within the womb, the first five or six years are usually considered the most formative in a child's life. Certainly this is an acknowledgment that what occurs on a physical, emotional, and spiritual basis during these first years leaves an indelible imprint on the child.

Deliberate Confusion of Memory

The more we learn about memory, the more our eyes are opened to its complexities. Understanding what happened during one's early years of life or in times of overwhelming trauma is not easy. To make matters worse, when ritual abuse is involved, perpetrators seem to make deliberate efforts to confuse and distort memory.

Costumes can be worn to confuse young children. Fake settings can be built.[52] Drugs, hypnosis, and other forms of illusion can further confound a child's perception. The primary purpose of many of these deliberate deceptions seems to be to trick children into believing things that are not true. This provides an excellent safeguard if the children should start remembering and disclosing what was done to them. Who is going to believe a child who says that Donald Duck did it or that it happened in the Amazon jungle?

Other more complex mind manipulations can seemingly be orchestrated by sophisticated cult perpetrators, such as separating the various sensory perceptions into different alter-identities or causing frequent switching so that each alter carries only a small segment of the event. Either of these techniques cause the memory to become like a jigsaw puzzle. The event can only be accurately recalled by bringing all of the alters involved in the event together at the same time so they can each recount their particular piece. Not only does this lessen the likelihood of the event being remembered, but this kind of memory can sometimes get reconstructed incorrectly, which again serves to confuse and discount belief in the reality of the event.

Cult perpetrators can also use guided imagery[53] or virtual reality to confuse a person's sense of reality. By bringing the individual, or a specific alter-identity, into an altered state of consciousness for such an experience, she may be unable to distinguish this artificially constructed episode from experience in the physical realm.

Through these various "artificial" means, perpetrators can implant into a survivor's mind many false beliefs concerning what actually happened to her. They can potentially use this to their advantage in a number of significant ways. In addition to intensifying intimidation, they could implicate innocent people as being involved in the cult, often those to whom the survivor might be tempted to disclose forbidden information or go to for help. They could also create scenarios designed to convince survivors that God is incapable or uninterested in helping them or fantasy situations defying the physical laws of nature in order to cause confusion and disbelief regarding the reality of their memories.

Being aware of these possible sources of confusion or deception regarding what is reported as "memory" is beneficial for both the survivor and those working with her as it provides an explanation for some purported "memories" which truly *do* seem impossible. This enables one to throw out *some* memories without having to throw them *all* out—as the perpetrators desire.

Validating Indicators of True Traumatic Memories

In light of all this potential confusion, questioning the veracity of specific recovered memories is certainly legitimate. Denying the phenomenon of recovered memories altogether is pure ignorance. In an effort to facilitate a knowledgeable evaluation of such memories, I would like to suggest a series of indicators that I believe serve to validate true Traumatic Memories.

The first is actual sensory replay when "remembering." If what is being recalled comes back as more than imagery in the head, that is, the person is not just visualizing scenes but is also "re-experiencing" other senses, such as touch, smell, or taste, you can know that that is a true Traumatic Memory because that is how Traumatic Memory is stored—in sensory form.[54] A memory that occurs in response to a trigger also bears the mark of a true Traumatic Memory since this is supposedly the only way dissociated Traumatic Memories can be accessed.

Another validating indicator is the simultaneous experience of some form of Body Memory symptoms as the event is recalled.

This may be the reappearance of specific injuries on the skin, the feeling of pain or pressure on the body, or virtually any other way in which body is activated as the memory is being recalled or discussed. Remember, the body is not suggestible.

The presence of supporting Implicit Memory is another validating indicator. In other words, effects in the person's life are consistent with the content of the memory. Sometimes the Implicit Memory effect is only recognized in retrospect as significant change occurs when healing is brought to the beliefs embedded in the memory.

Along a similar line, if God is called upon to speak truth into these beliefs and He does so in an undisputable way, I believe that can also validate the reality of a memory. I do not believe that God would respond to inaccurate or imaginative "memories."

If the memory reveals content the person could not have otherwise known, that is also a validating indicator. For instance, if such things as crematorium furnaces or specific surgical instruments appear in a memory of a person who has had no reason to have encountered such things, this would lend considerable credibility to the memory. A person cannot accurately imagine something she has never seen.

If the content of the memory includes an element of surprise, something that would never have been imagined, this too lends support to the genuineness of the memory. Obviously, supporting physical evidence provides perhaps the most concrete indicator of a memory's reality.

Memories of guided imagery or virtual reality experiences are also of real events. They can be extremely traumatic and thus produce Implicit Memory effects and some of these other characteristics as well. However, experiences that did not involve the body cannot produce true Body Memories. Sensory replay would also be impossible for guided imagery memories.

Supposed "memories" arising purely from one's imagination will bear none of these validating indicators. That does not mean, however, that all memories lacking any of the above characteristics are imaginary. They just need to be considered "iffy." In time, some of them may be confirmed. Drawing conclusions or making major decisions on these kinds of "memories" would not be wise, however.

The emotional reaction a person has in response to a "memory" is not a valid indicator of its reality. Imagined scenarios can activate one's emotions as well as real ones. Movies and guided imagery experiences can be real "tear-jerkers." Reading or listening to scary stories can stimulate children's imaginations and arouse considerable fear in them.

Conclusion

What scientists know about the neurobiology of memory is fascinating but incomplete. Even if the memory data stored in the brain could be precisely extracted, it can only be viewed or experienced on a conscious level through the filter of the mind. The role of the mind in interacting with this material cannot be eliminated. What the mind does with what is or is not recorded in the brain is an uncontrollable "wild card." Rarely will the memory data emerge "untouched."

The bottom line is that understanding and evaluating memory is not an exact science. Narrative Memory is easily distorted. Traumatic Memory, while accurate and at times verifiable, is at best sketchy. Implicit Memory and Body Memory are infallible but non-verbal.

This need not impede healing, however. God desires us to know "truth in [our] innermost being" (Ps. 51:6). "He knows what is in the darkness" and is able to "reveal the hidden things" (Dan 2:22; NASB) from our personal histories that need to be healed. He can bring what is in the darkness into the light.

While some things, such as correctly identifying one's perpetrators, are vitally important, knowing every detail of one's traumatic history is not critical to healing. What is essential is identifying the *beliefs* that one carried out of the traumatic events, whatever they were. Bringing truth to those painful and often debilitating false beliefs is the truth that sets a person free (John 8:32)!

Endnotes

[1] Bessel A. van der Kolk, Alexander C. McFarlane, and Lars Weisaeth, eds., *Traumatic Stress: The Effects of Overwhelming Experience on Mind, Body, and Society* (New York: Guildford Press, 1996), x.

[2] Ibid., 308.

[3] Richard Horevitz, "Hypnosis in the Treatment of Multiple Personality Disorder," *Handbook of Clinical Hypnosis,* eds. Rhue, Lynn, and Kirsch (American Psychological Association), 19.

[4] Bessel A. van der Kolk, "Trauma, Consciousness, and the Body," Harvard Medical College Continuing Education Course, Longboat Key, FL, Feb. 2003.

[5] Horevitz, 20.

[6] Bessel A. van der Kolk and Onno van der Hart, "The Intrusive Past: The Flexibility of Memory and the Engraving of Trauma," *American Imago* 48, 4 (1991), 436.

[7] Bessel A. van der Kolk, "Trauma, Memory, and the Integration of Experience," ISSD Regional Conference, Washington, DC, 1996.

[8] Ibid.

[9] van der Kolk, "The Intrusive Past," 439.

[10] Ibid., 427.

[11] van der Kolk, "Trauma, Memory, and the Integration of Experience."

[12] Ibid.

[13] Ibid.

[14] Ibid.

[15] van der Kolk, "The Intrusive Past," 427.

[16] van der Kolk, "Trauma, Memory, and Integration of Experience."

[17] DSM-IV Field Trials (1991), reported by van der Kolk, "The Intrusive Past," 443.

[18] van der Kolk, *Traumatic Stress*, 282.

[19] van der Kolk, "Trauma, Memory, and the Integration of Experience."

[20] van der Kolk, "The Intrusive Past," 440.

[21] Ibid., 427.

[22] DSM-IV Field Trials (1991), reported by van der Kolk, "The Intrusive Past," 443.

[23] van der Kolk, "Trauma, Memory, and the Integration of Experience."

[24] van der Kolk, "The Intrusive Past," 431-32.

[25] Ibid., 431.

[26] van der Kolk, *Traumatic Stress,* 287, 312.

[27] Ibid., 312.

[28] van der Kolk, "Trauma, Consciousness, and the Body."

[29] van der Kolk, "The Intrusive Past," 441.

[30] Ibid.

[31] Ibid., 431.

[32] Ibid.

[33] Ibid., 442.

[34] Ibid., 431.

[35] van der Kolk, *Traumatic Stress,* 296-97.

[36] Ibid., 313.

[37] van der Kolk, "The Intrusive Past," 427.

[38] van der Kolk, *Traumatic Stress,* 297.

[39] van der Kolk, "The Intrusive Past," 427.

[40] Janina Fisher, "Trauma, Consciousness, and the Body," Harvard Medical College Continuing Education Course, Longboat Key, FL, Feb. 2003.

[41] Ibid.

[42] van der Kolk, "The Intrusive Past," 443.

[43] van der Kolk, *Traumatic Stress,* 290.

[44] Ibid., 217.

[45] Ibid., 219-20, 280.

[46] Ibid., 214.

[47] van der Kolk, "The Intrusive Past," 442.

[48] Thomas Verny with John Kelly, *The Secret Life of the Unborn Child* (New York: Dell Trade Paperback, 1981), 23.

[49] Ibid., 102; David Kleinschuster, personal communication, July 2003.

[50] Wendy Anne McCarty, "The Power of Beliefs: What Babies are Teaching Us," *Journal of Prenatal & Perinatal Psychology & Health* 16, 4 (Summer 2002), *353*-56.

[51] John and Paula Sandford, *Healing Prenatal Wounds and Sins,* videocassette (Ontario: Mainroads Production, 1985).

[52] Jerry Mungadze reports that a ritual site was found in Texas that was made to look like the Amazon jungle.

[53] *Goddess Rituals and Meditations* (no further publication data recalled).

[54] van der Kolk, *Traumatic Stress,* 288-89.

Chapter Five

The Role of Conflict and Denial in DID

Understanding the role that conflict plays in the dynamics of DID will greatly enhance your ability to interact with a multiple's system of alter-identities in a manner that is most conducive to her healing. It will help you appreciate the distinct perspectives and roles of the alters and know how to validate them in an appropriate way that facilitates the eventual removal of the dissociative walls rather than strengthening them.

The Creation of Dissociative Barriers

DID is created in a child's mind as a means to cope with intolerable psychic distress. Once the level of psychic distress caused by a traumatic event surpasses the child's threshold of tolerance, dissociation may occur, shifting consciousness away from the Core Self to a separate area of the brain.

This "problem-solving" area of the brain must find a way to cope with the inescapable impact of the traumatic event. Usually this means addressing and resolving what is perceived as an intolerable psychological conflict arising from the event. In children who have been repeatedly traumatized from a very young age, a further separation of consciousness may occur and distinct alter-identities formed. Each one will be carefully designed to eliminate or drastically reduce the perceived intolerable conflict.

The dissociative walls separating these alter-identities from the Core Self will remain until the intolerable conflicts seemingly necessitating them are identified and addressed. For this reason understanding the nature of intolerable conflicts and their role in the formation of alter-identities is essential if the need for the dissociative barriers is ever to be eliminated.

Psychological conflicts exist whenever a person feels two or more opposing instincts, needs, feelings, desires, beliefs, views of reality, or impulses at the same time. For instance, a working mother waking up to find her child is sick is torn between needing to be at home to care for her child and needing to be at work to complete a special project. Another type of conflict arises when a person carrying a deep spiritual commitment to honesty gets a badly needed job only to find that his boss expects him to alter figures in a critical financial report. Conflicts such as these are normal occurrences in life and, while uncomfortable, are usually manageable by a mature adult.

Intolerable conflicts occur when an encountered situation threatens a critical instinct, need, belief, or view of reality which seems *inviolable.* For instance, all human beings, even before birth, carry a very strong survival instinct. Therefore, any event that seems to threaten this instinct will create an intolerable conflict. If the child is young enough, her psyche may respond by using dissociation to separate her Core Self from the threatening reality. This allows the Core to maintain her confidence in survival while an alter-identity holds the reality of the trauma and the recognition that her survival may indeed be jeopardized.

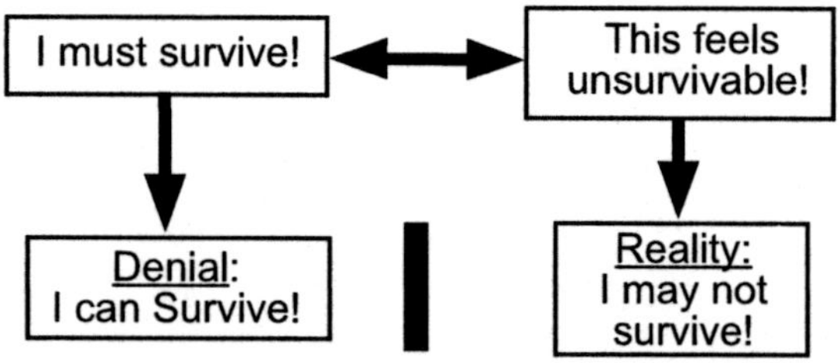

Figure 1: Survival Conflict

If you can grasp the mechanism of how this most foundational conflict can cause dissociative barriers to be erected within the child's mind, you will readily recognize that whenever such a child believes that she is in an unsurvivable situation, she will use dissociation, or "splitting," to protect her Core Self from knowledge of the event so that this primary identity can maintain her confidence of survival. The more the child is placed in situations that threaten this critical belief, the more alter-identities she may create to encapsulate the trauma away from her normal stream of consciousness.

The need to attach to a parent or primary caretaker is another powerful instinct in an infant or small child. This too can be intolerably threatened when the parent or caretaker is extremely abusive. Again, the level of psychic distress caused by this conflict may result in dissociation so that the Core Self can be separated from the abuse and thus able to maintain the belief that the parent is good. She is then able to attach to the abusive parent figure while another part of her has to cope with the reality that the parent is evil, untrustworthy, and dangerous.

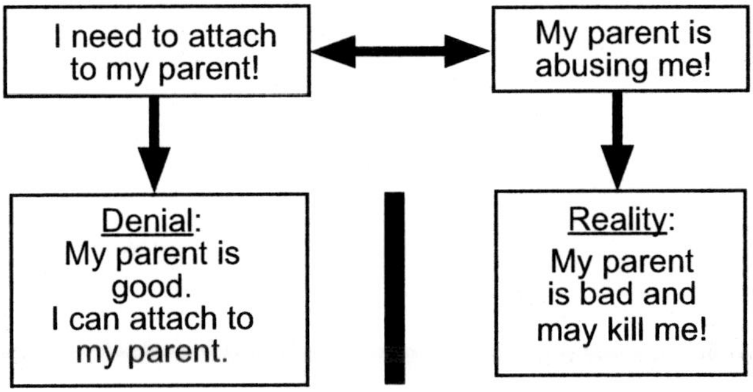

Figure 2: Attachment Conflict

This conflict explains why some identities will usually have warm feelings towards the parent or caretaker, no matter how despicable he or she is/was. Sometimes factors are present, however, which preclude any type of healthy attachment to the parent or caretaker, resulting in attachment disorders.

Abused children generally face many other conflicts that seem just as intolerable. Once they have begun to use dissociation at an early age to resolve them, their psyches will usually revert to this same defensive mechanism to cope with these conflicts as well, splitting themselves again and again in order to isolate whatever is viewed as intolerable away from the Core Self so she does not have to "own" such realities.

For instance, as these children mature, they will eventually be required to take on increasing responsibilities in caring for themselves, participating in family life, doing chores, and going to school. The problem is that the trauma-bearing alters which they have already created are generally too laden down with the emotional impact of the abuse to be able to function normally in these situations. This leaves the burden to do so on the "unabused" Core.

By this time, however, the psyche may perceive that the child's environment is too risky and unpredictable to allow the Core Self to be directly involved in it at all. This creates the intolerable conflict of the Core simultaneously needing to function in external life and to be protected from it.

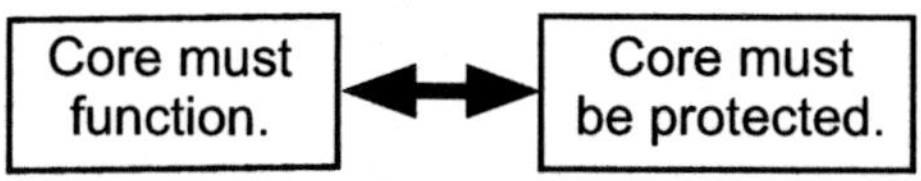

Figure 3: Function Conflict

At this point a further level of dissociation may occur with another major dissociative split occurring seemingly directly from the Core. The newly formed identity remains just as separated from the knowledge and implications of the trauma as the Core, enabling her to function well in external life. This major new identity is called the "Host" and, while directly related to the Core, functions separately from her. The Host will essentially represent the Core in "normal" life experiences.

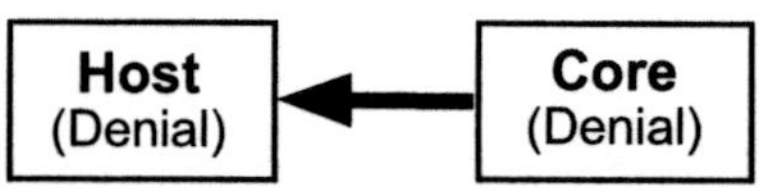

Figure 4: Creation of the Host

The Host may form additional alters to help with specific aspects of everyday life. For instance, one may handle going to school, another doing chores, and another preparing for bed, etc. Sometimes the Host splits off alters who are designed to encapsulate and preserve seemingly treasured abilities, such as special artistic talents or even just the ability to have fun, if these things seem to be threatened. All of the alters created by the Host will be as unaware of the trauma as she is. Together with the Host, they form what is called the "Presenter System."

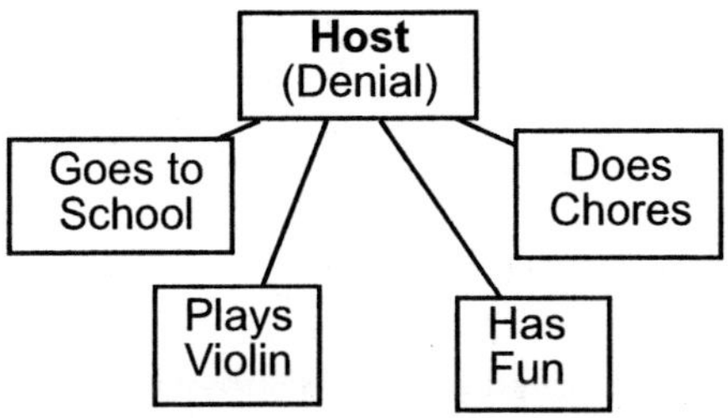

Figure 5: Creation of the Presenter System

This has now effectively divided the psyche of the child into three major components: the Core, who is highly invested in denial for the purpose of survival; the Host and Presenter System, who are highly invested in denial for the purpose of functioning; and the many alter-identities who are highly invested in containing the trauma memories so that the Core and the Host can maintain the illusion that no abuse happened.

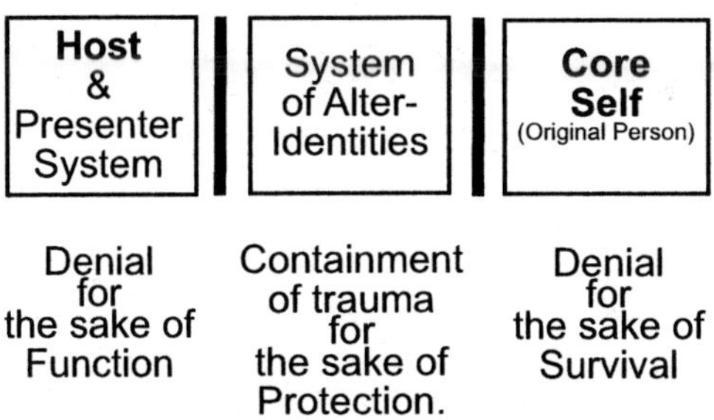

Adapted from David Neswald

Figure 6: Core Preservation Model

Multiplicity can thus be seen as a massive defense mechanism designed to protect both the Core and the Host from knowledge of the trauma. Virtually all multiples will exhibit these three major divisions in their psyches since the underlying conflicts which create them are generally universal in cases of repeated, severe abuse.[1]

Other intolerable conflicts causing further splitting of the psyche will depend on the particular circumstances the individual encounters. Some of these conflicts will arise naturally out of the abusive environment. Others may be deliberately orchestrated by knowledgeable perpetrators who desire to produce the strong dissociative (and amnesic) barriers which result from such conflicts and are essential for keeping their immoral activities hidden from the Host.

Safety is always a paramount concern of abused children. Therefore, significant conflicts may arise over what is perceived to be necessary in order to be safe. If the slightest misperformance brings severe punishment, the child may come to believe that she must be "perfect" in order to be safe while at the same time recognizing that she cannot possibly meet this impossible performance standard. The intolerable nature of this conflict may potentially lead to a series of dissociative splits, resulting in alter-identities who carry a variety of perspectives.

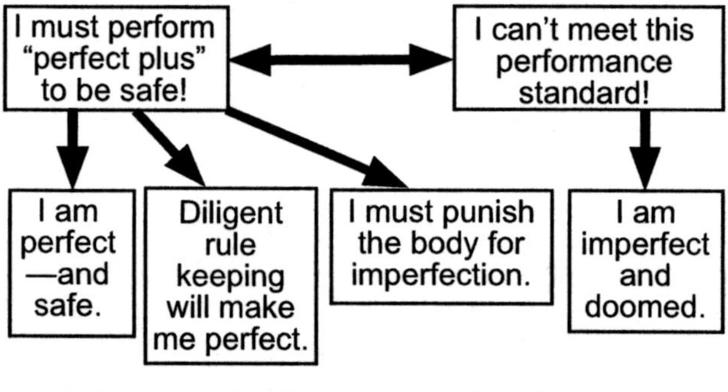

Figure 7: Performance/Safety Conflict

First of all, the conflict usually results in the creation of an alter who believes that she is truly perfect—and thus safe. In order to maintain her illusion of safety, she only experiences life when the person's behavior is truly in line with the perceived requirements of the perpetrator(s). As soon as any hint of doing something "wrong" occurs, she is immediately removed from participation in life so that she doesn't have to "own" the imperfect behavior. This alter usually reflects a strong and confident self-image, perhaps accompanied by some veiled feelings of superiority. These are understandable, however, when you realize the nature of the conflict out of which she was created and the absolute necessity of her having this view of herself in order to be safe.

This powerful performance conflict may also result in one or more alters adopting the belief that "diligent rule-keeping will make me perfect—and thus safe." These alters may become compulsively devoted to an ever-increasing list of rules gleaned from an astute observation of the actions of other people, especially their perpetrators. Practically every aspect of life may become governed by these rigid, often self-imposed, directives, which gain their strength from the deep conviction that safety will be assured if the child can just do everything "right."

This conflict may also produce alters who become self-punishers. They will actually hurt the body when the Host, or whoever is in control, breaks a "rule" or does something "wrong." The inflicted injury is intended to warn the erring parts to "shape up" so that they don't experience more serious punishment from the perpetrator(s).

Finally, this conflict often results in the creation of an alter to embody the unbearable reality that the child is truly imperfect and thus doomed to inevitable failure and punishment. This part often exhibits a fatalistic gloom and may easily become suicidal.

If the child is also severely *shamed* for not performing well enough, her sense of inherent "goodness" as a person may also become tied to the unattainable performance standard. In this case the conflict may produce the same kinds of alters mentioned above, but the alter who bears the reality of her imperfection often believes that she is totally "bad" and unworthy of life. She feels like "garbage" because that is exactly how her perpetrator(s) have treated her, and she has had to bear the brunt of it. She too may very understandably become suicidal.

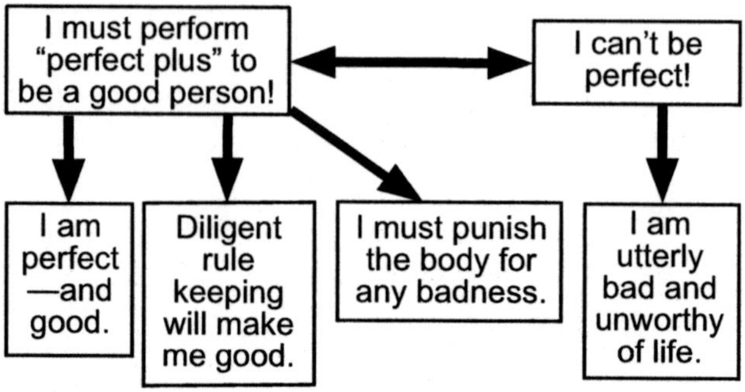

Figure 8: Performance/Goodness Conflict

Unfortunately, the control of emotions often becomes a safety issue as well. How can abused children possibly avoid having extreme emotional reactions to the abuse they experience? At the same time they usually know very well that expressing any of these inevitable emotions will result in further trauma.

This intolerable conflict can also be resolved through dissociation. By creating a separate alter to contain the forbidden emotion, other identities can appear emotion-free—and thus be safe. This dissociative maneuver can be used to provide separation from virtually any intolerable or unacceptable emotions, such as anger, pain, shame, or guilt. This dynamic explains why some survivors may seem unusually devoid of emotions, even in very disturbing situations. It also explains why some alters may seem virtually consumed with a particular emotion. Containing this emotion may be their sole purpose.

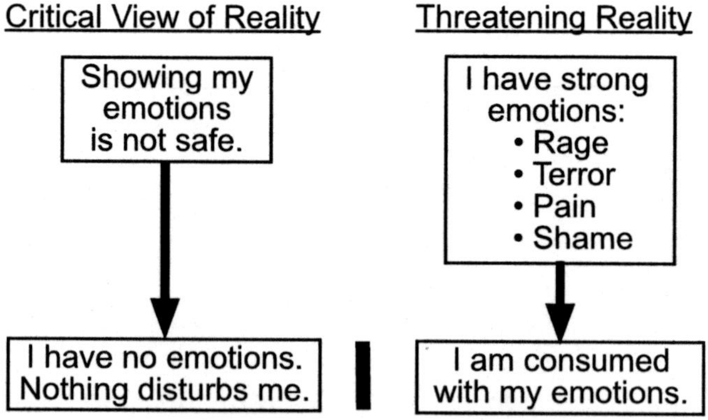

Figure 9: Emotions Conflict

Other intolerable conflicts arise when the person is forced to participate in activities which are totally against the moral standards or spiritual commitments of the Core. In this case dissociation will typically be used to create an identity to embody the absolutely unacceptable activity (e.g., illicit sex, perpetrator acts, or criminal activity) so the Core and Host can maintain the belief that they do not do such things and thus preserve a sense of personal morality and dignity as well as assurance of their acceptance by God.

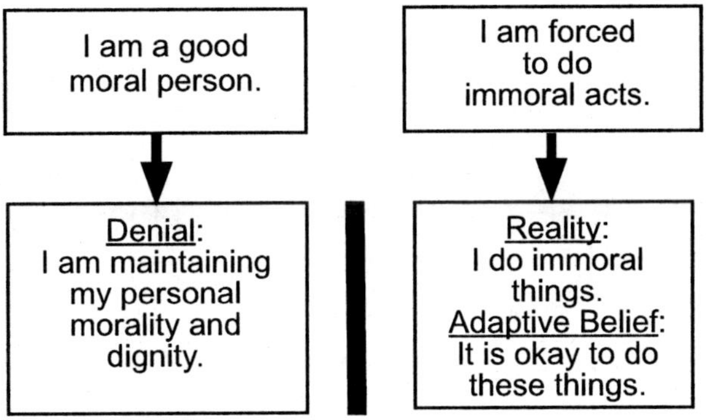

Figure 10: Moral Identity Conflict

The alter embodying the immoral behavior will generally adopt a non-dissociative means to lessen its repulsive impact, perhaps finding a way to justify the belief system of the perpetrator(s). When you meet this alter, she may seem to have a seared conscience, and you may be tempted to judge her for her immoral perspectives or behavior. If you understand the intolerable conflict which her existence is serving to resolve, however, and how this protects the Core from owning what is so objectionable to her, you will be much more apt to treat her with compassion. The truth is that her very existence speaks to the extent of the Core's commitment *not* to engage in such activity.

Because sophisticated cult perpetrators seem to understand the role of conflict in producing dissociation, they often intentionally create intolerable conflicts for the children they are grooming for their purposes. They are extremely adept at this, realizing that the more intense the conflict, the stronger will be the dissociative (and amnesic) barriers erected to separate the alters embodying the intolerable reality from the Core and Host.

This is perhaps why they like to work with children from Christian homes. The stronger a person's Christian commitment is, the stronger will be the dissociative barriers erected to separate the Core and Host from those identities that are forced into immoral, criminal, or Satanic activity—which is exactly what the perpetrators want in order to keep their cover in place. From these "disowned" and separated identities they can then build entire systems of alters that they can manipulate to serve their own purposes.

If the child's parents are themselves cult members or cooperative with the cult agenda, they can manipulate many formative dynamics in the child's home life to set her up for intolerable conflicts. This is truly the most ideal way to get deeply embedded belief systems established in the child's mind. Among other things, the parents can purposely set extremely high performance standards and then severely shame and punish the child when she fails to meet them, setting up the intolerable performance conflict described above.

They can also teach the child extremely high moral standards and severely condemn anyone who does not practice them. This will again set the child up for an intolerable conflict when the cult later forces her into activities which violate those standards.

Parents can also manipulate their child's spiritual beliefs, taking her to a church which defines sin with a long list of rules and delivers "hellfire and damnation" preaching against sin. This sets the child up for an intolerable conflict when the cult forces her to violate God's commandments, supposedly acquiring His wrath and being condemned to hell.

Even if cult perpetrators do not have access to the child's home environment, they can still manipulate abusive situations to produce the dissociative barriers they desire. One usually effective means of doing so is to subject the child to survival threatening experiences, preferably beginning at a pre-verbal age. The child's critical need to preserve confidence in her ability to survive will usually induce the dissociative response the perpetrator(s) desire.

Another way is to engage dissociative individuals in extremely terrifying, humiliating, or incriminating acts. If the resulting level of terror, shame, or guilt reaches an intolerable level, it will create intense motivation to dissociate from the events and never remove the dissociative barriers—which would mean re-encountering the intolerable emotions.

When survivors report memories of seemingly pointless torture or humiliation, you may wonder why perpetrators would do such inhumane things to children. The truth is that most of these activities are probably not done for sadistic pleasure. Instead, the goal is to evoke intolerable emotions and conflicts, which will enhance dissociation and enable the cult to accomplish their *real* agenda behind the amnesic barriers created by these unbearable experiences.

When females reach puberty, cult perpetrators may deliberately impregnate them in order to use the powerful mother-child bond to create further intolerable conflicts in them. Killing or sacrificing the child before the mother's eyes will generally create a strong need for her to dissociate the intolerable event into another alter. If she is made to sacrifice the child herself, the need for dissociation will be even more intense, and the alter formed to embody the event will be separated from the rest of the person by an exceptionally strong amnesic barrier so that she never has to encounter the intolerable pain and guilt connected to that act.

Once dissociative barriers are erected to resolve an intolerable conflict, they will remain until the beliefs seemingly necessitating them are identified, challenged, and adjusted to reflect truth and eliminate the intolerable conflict. This must be a primary objective of the therapy process.

The Role of Denial

Understanding the role that intolerable conflicts play in establishing dissociative barriers hopefully enables you to see that *the need to deny reality* is what actually drives the dissociative process. In severe cases the child is placed in one intolerable situation after another. The result is that she needs to deny reality in order to preserve her confidence in survival, her sense of safety, her moral identity, and her acceptance to God as well as to enable her attachment to abusive parents, her ability to function, and her separation from intolerable emotions.

This overwhelming need for denial plays a significant role not only in the creation of the dissociative walls but also in maintaining their ongoing existence. We might say that denial is the "glue" that holds the dissociation in place.

Unfortunately, too many therapists have treated denial as merely an annoyance to brush aside rather than recognizing the key role that it plays in the entire dissociative process. The truth is that DID would not exist without the mind's seeming need for denial. This means that when denial is no longer needed, neither is dissociation.

Letting go of one's denial is not as easy as it may sound, however. In fact, the survivor's journey out of denial usually occurs in a gradual manner. At first the presenting Host may deny even being multiple. When she can no longer deny the existence of her alter-identities, she may still deny the allegations of abuse they carry.

As the reality of abuse slowly sinks in, she may reluctantly accept it, but on an incremental basis as well. For instance, she may begin by accepting physical abuse but not sexual abuse, then sexual abuse but not ritual abuse, or abuse by her father but not by her mother.

Eventually *all* the abuse from *all* the perpetrators may be accepted, but the Core and the Host may still resist "owning" those experiences, preferring them to continue to be held by the alter-identities. Somehow being separated from them still seems more advantageous than being united with them.

Only when the Core Self is willing to *own* the previously denied events can the dissociative walls come down. This is why the therapeutic focus belongs much more heavily on the Core and her upfront representative, the Host, than previously recognized. These key identities must identify and resolve the conflicts and beliefs that originally seemed to necessitate denial as well as those that make it seem advantageous in the present.

A survivor's ongoing investment in denial and dissociation as an adult may at first seem strange. Consider, however, the magnitude of the impact that giving up her protected, dissociated state will have on her.

Her whole sense of identity will have to undergo radical changes, This does not come easily after living for decades with a certain perception. Her struggles in this area may encompass not only critical moral and spiritual issues but also concerns involving her personality, her functionality, her rationality, her family image, and her worldview. Because the changes she must make in each of these areas strike so deeply into the very essence of who she is, they can be extremely difficult for her to embrace.

If the Host sees herself as a self-confident and outgoing person, she may resist owning the parts of her that are depressed and withdrawn. Likewise, if she views herself as a highly competent person, she may not want to accept parts that seem weak or confused or that struggle to get things done.

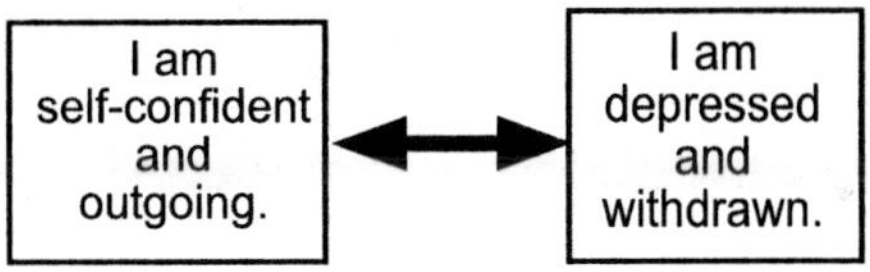

Figure 11: Personality Conflict

For many high functioning multiples the fear of compromising their performance capabilities can be a major obstacle keeping them from embracing wholeness. They may believe that integration would result in a blending of the function levels of all their identities. They fail to realize that in integration the ego strengths of the alter-identities, however great or small they may be, will be *added* to that of the Core Self, making her even stronger.

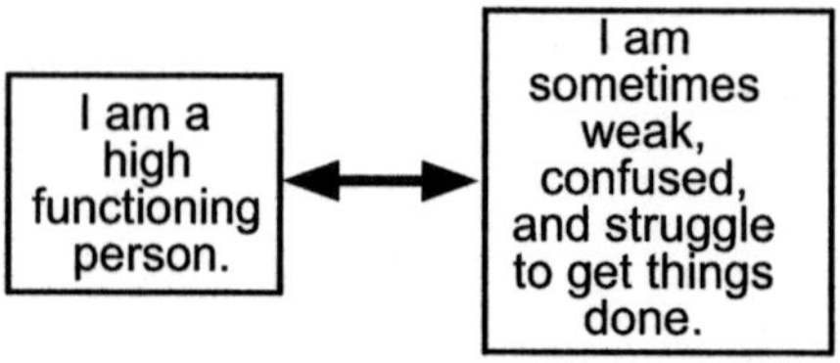

Figure 12: Functionality Conflict

Rationality can also be a strongly valued component of some survivors' identities, especially those who have been educated in a scientific field. Discovering the totality of who they are and embracing a hidden part of their history will require them to move way outside their comfort zones. While being accustomed to determining reality through physical evidence, they will have to begin trusting what their minds, emotions, and bodies are telling them, often without any other clear evidence.

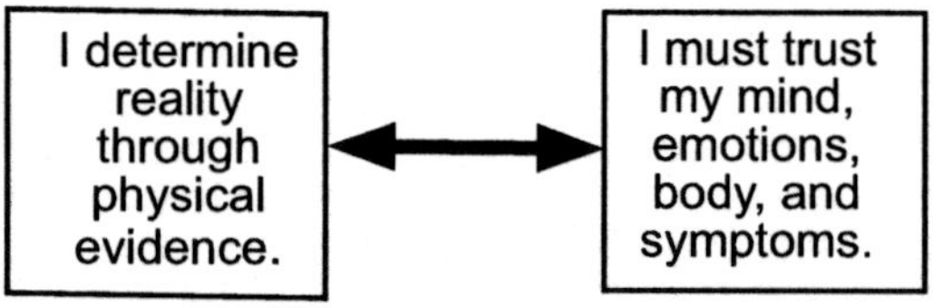

Figure 13: Rationality Conflict

Rewriting one's autobiography of life to contain unspeakable abuse may deeply impact the image the survivor has of her childhood and her family. Because she is an extension of her family, this too is an identity issue. Coming to grips with the reality that she was betrayed by those who gave her birth and were supposed to love and protect her can be especially difficult.

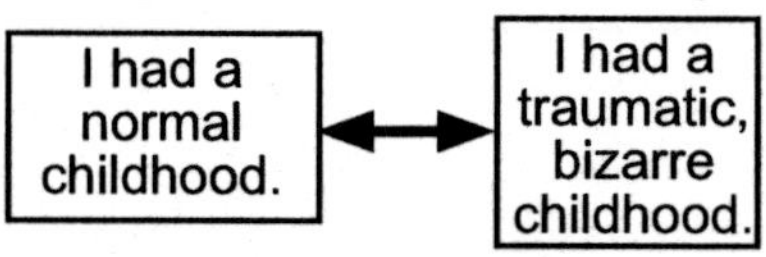

Figure 14: Nature of Childhood Conflict

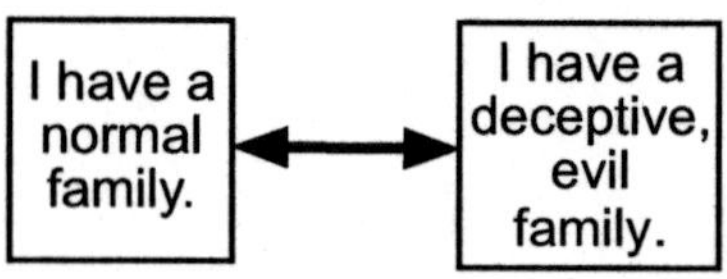

Figure 15: Family Image Conflict

One of the biggest identity conflicts for many survivors concerns the issue of morality. How does a person who has committed herself to high moral and godly standards own the fact that she has done unspeakably evil and immoral acts? When a survivor not only is committed to such standards but also believes she has been successful in maintaining them, embracing these sordid realities of her past can be extremely difficult.

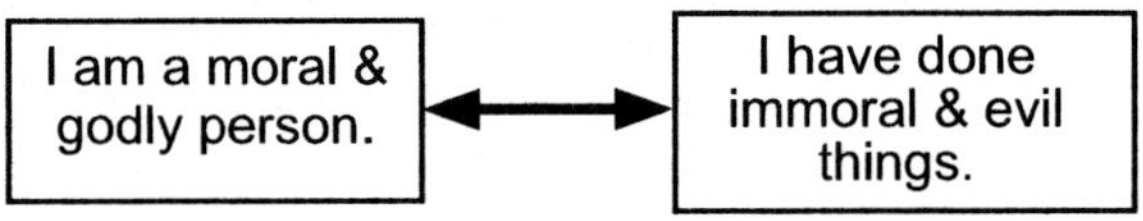

Figure 16: Personal Morality Conflict

For a ritual abuse survivor, the challenge of owning her entire history is even greater as it may mean owning the realities of having unknown children, being connected to an evil network, being programmed for evil purposes, being demonized, or engaging in activity in the occult realm. Avoiding these realities can be a powerful incentive to hold onto denial.

Other undesirable identity issues include the stigma of needing prolonged treatment within the mental health community or of having a sometimes "controversial" diagnosis. If the survivor does own her diagnosis and her history, she must resign herself either to live the rest of her life carrying a huge secret about herself or to face the risk of rejection and misunderstanding if she should disclose it. In all reality, she will probably be unable to be completely real and open with all but perhaps a few select people.

If she accepts her true history, she may also need to make significant changes in her relationships and her lifestyle, perhaps separating from her family and even moving to a different part of the country. She will also have to adopt a significantly different view of the world and become much more suspicious and vigilant of what is going on around her.

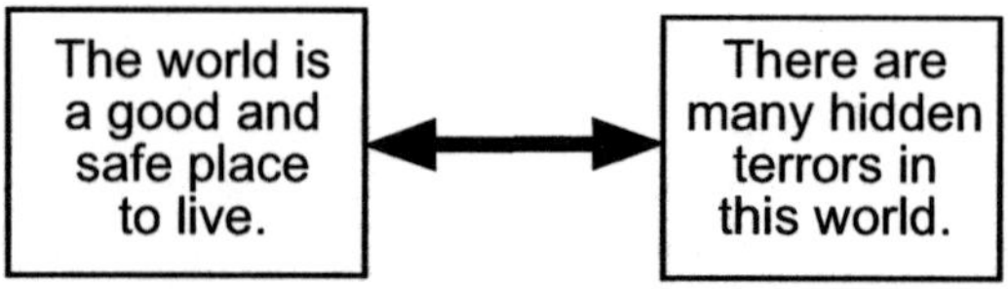

Figure 17: Worldview Conflict

Another powerful motivator for keeping dissociation in place is the ability to maintain the separation from pain and other intolerable emotions that it enables. In order to achieve wholeness a survivor must find some benefit in owning her entire history that surpasses her fear of confronting these emotions.

Denial and dissociation also provides a way for those survivors who are devoted Christians to maintain certain godly commitments. For most Christians, sexual immorality is a paramount sin, to say nothing of betraying God, participating in Satanic activities, and engaging in occult access to the spiritual realm. These things are totally incompatible with Christianity! They are unthinkable! For this reason Satanically abused Christians face enormous hurdles in being willing to remove the dissociative barriers and own their entire history.

On the other hand, a Christian survivor has the tremendous advantage of being able to bring God into the healing journey. When sought, His divine perspective can marvelously eliminate the intolerable nature of whatever conflict the survivor faces. As God is able to convey directly to her that He knows her heart and does not judge her for actions that parts of her were coerced into performing, He can totally melt their resistance to owning even the most ungodly experiences.

His love and guidance throughout the healing process is absolutely invaluable! In fact, if survivors will allow Him to do so, God's truth and wisdom can enable them to overcome all of their seemingly good reasons for remaining divided. He has a wonderful way for them to be at peace with themselves and their entire histories.

Overcoming Denial and Dissociation

Overcoming denial and becoming whole is not just a matter of knowing what to do to get there. It takes considerable ego strength, motivation and courage. The truth is that not all survivors may have these in sufficient degree. Having a supportive relationship along the journey, however, can be of immense help in building these crucial elements and the capacity to be able to encounter what was previously so overwhelming that it had to be hidden behind dissociative barriers.[2]

Motivation is a key factor that must be carefully understood. Being dedicated to therapy and to the *idea* of becoming whole is not enough. Going to therapy is easy! Becoming whole is not!

Survivors may readily desire the advantages of wholeness, such as relief from unpleasant symptoms, improved functionality and relationships, knowing truth, and making sense out of their lives. Each one must critically evaluate, however, whether she is truly willing to pay the price to achieve these goals. Is she willing to go through intensive therapy and the many discomforts of change? Is she willing to confront painful memories and seemingly intolerable emotions? Is she willing to embrace her entire history and all the implications that it carries in regard to her identity, her image, her family, and her worldview?

Is Wholeness Worth the Price?

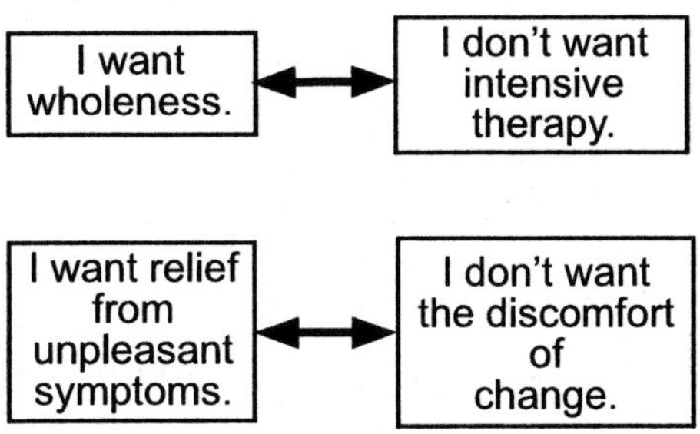

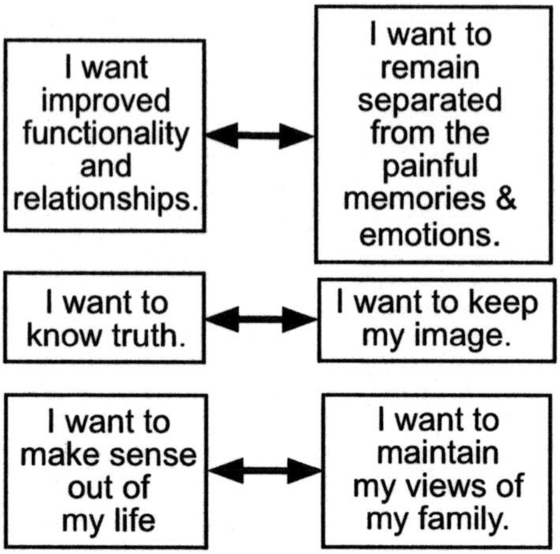

Figure 18: Motivation Conflicts

The survivor who can find a reason to pursue wholeness that surpasses the advantages of remaining divided and is willing to "pay the price" must still be prepared to embark upon a very courageous journey. Initially, she will have to relinquish the control that has seemed so vital to her safety and risk vulnerability in order for the healing process to even begin. She will have to dare to begin to trust again and to be willing to let another person into the hidden areas of her innermost self and all the secrets that reside there.

She will have to overcome her fears and embrace the truth and all of its implications, relinquishing her cherished image of herself and be willing to embrace a new image. She will have to let go of a dissociated and protected way of life that has served her so well in many regards and be willing to embark upon a new and unknown way of living.

If she is a ritual abuse survivor, she will have to walk bravely in the face of life-threatening terror and the all-pervasive threats designed to keep her submissive to cult control for life and be willing to trust God her life instead. She will also have to confront the spiritual forces of darkness with which she may have unknowingly become entwined and trust God for victory.

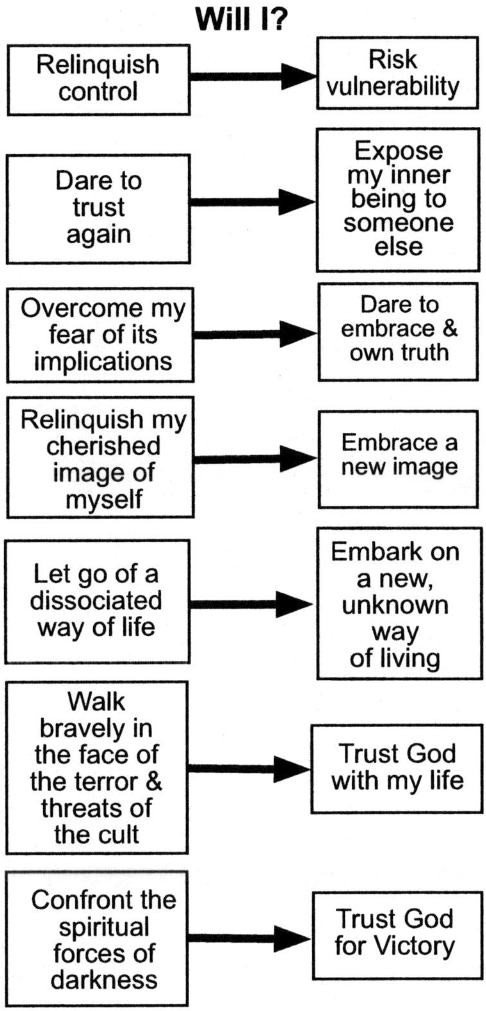

Figure 19: Courage Issues

Acquiring sufficient ego strength, motivation, and courage is the difficult part of becoming whole. The actual process of addressing the denial and dissociation is relatively easy. The key is to identify the *beliefs* that underlie the seeming need for denial. A critical question to ask is "What would it mean if these things were true?" This will require some deep introspection for the survivor, who must totally ignore what her adult, rational mind believes and seek the answer from deep within on an emotional level.

When the belief is identified, the survivor must remain in contact with this deep inner part of her being and be willing to have the truth of the belief challenged. Often this can be done by asking God to reveal His perspective on it. When this is successful and God reveals His truth, the event may immediately lose its intolerable nature, and the dissociative walls seemingly necessitated because of the false belief will no longer be needed. In many cases they will spontaneously disintegrate.

If this does not occur, additional beliefs may need to be identified and addressed or the Core Self (or the representative Host) was not truly involved in the process. All of the dissociative walls serve to protect the Core Self. Therefore, they cannot be removed without this essential part of the person embracing truth.

As the walls begin to come down and the survivor starts claiming more and more of her true self, she will experience a deep sense of "rightness" about the process. This will help to propel her forward until she is completely whole.

Implications for Relationship

Understanding the role of conflict and denial in DID carries some significant implications regarding relating to survivors and their alter-identities. How you do this can have a profound impact on either strengthening or weakening the internal conflicts and thus the need for the dissociative barriers.

A key principle in regard to any conflict is that the stronger one side advances its position or beliefs, the stronger the other side will retaliate in asserting its position. For instance, anything that serves to support the allegations of those alters holding the memories of the abuse will cause the parts invested in denial to proclaim their disbelief even more strongly. If they are too threatened, they may even take drastic actions to protect their position, such as breaking off relationships with those trying to help them or even withdrawing from therapy.

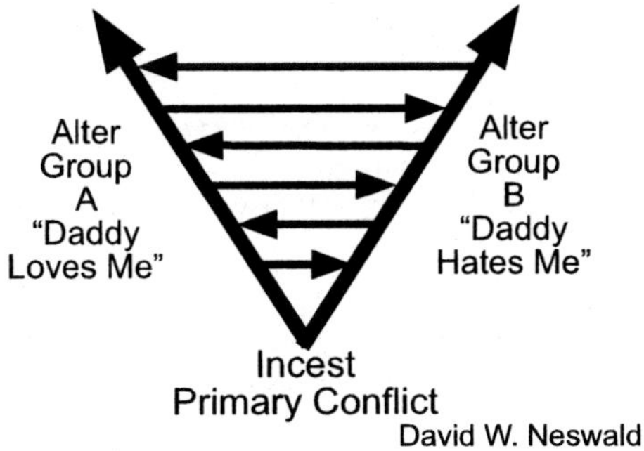

Figure 20: Schizmogenesis Model

Therefore, you must be careful not to express your support for any particular side of a conflict too strongly or to cast blame on another. Whenever you give the impression that one side is "right" and the other "wrong," you strengthen the conflict and the ongoing need for dissociation.

As much as possible show equal respect to all identities regardless of their stated beliefs and behaviors. Avoid labels which subtly imply judgment, such as "light side" or "dark side." Be particularly careful not to support any part's condemnation of "sinful" alters. Not only will this strengthen the internal walls, but it may also drive the scorned ones into deeper hiding, which is counterproductive to healing. Instead, convey a willingness to hear the perspectives of all parts.

Because these conflict-reducing responses are often the opposite of what comes naturally, don't expect immediate perfection from yourself. Once you experience the positive results of affirming all identities equally, including those that are cult-aligned or invested in denial, you will become steadily more proficient in developing these skills, resulting in significant benefit to the survivor.

Endnotes

[1] Tom Hawkins reports that he often finds a "Buffer" Identity situated between the Core and the Host Identities. He refers to these identities as Primary Parts.

[2] James Wilder, Thrive Conference, Baldwin, MI, Oct. 2002.

Chapter Six

Emotional Support

Supporting an abuse survivor through the emotional throes of her recovery process is one of the most appreciated and healing forms of support you can offer. It is probably the most challenging and potentially draining to the supporter as well.

Those able to assist in this area need a good grasp of the dynamics of trauma, emotions, and dissociation as well as a special sensitivity to hurting people. They must be able to show genuine compassion while maintaining objectivity and healthy boundaries. They also need substantial inner fortitude to handle hearing hideous, gruesome, and perverted memories and to interact with the survivor's wide range of emotions and personalities.

Providing emotional support does not need to be an all-or-nothing situation, however. You may be able to provide significant love, compassion, and moral support even if you prefer not to listen to the actual memories. This is perfectly acceptable but should be communicated to the survivor up front.

If you *are* willing to accompany the survivor as she revisits the unbearable memories of her past, however, your presence alone will speak volumes, contrasting greatly with the utter abandonment she felt when the events originally took place. Your compassion will be like a medicinal balm to her inner wounds, and she will finally receive what she so badly needed and deserved as a child.

Because the mind will only release its painful, hidden secrets if it senses that the person is in a safe and supportive environment, you may be the key, in fact, that unlocks this important door that is so crucial to her healing. If you also learn how to identify the beliefs causing the pain and to bring healing to those wounds once they are exposed (see pp. 77-80), you will be of invaluable assistance to her.

The Nature of Repressed Emotions

Abuse invariably evokes intense emotions, no matter how or when it is inflicted. When it occurs in childhood, however, the individual generally lacks the opportunity to express or process those emotions as they arise. The perpetrator is too powerful. If the child were to react in anger or cry out in pain, she might risk greater punishment or torture. Furthermore, any possibility of seeking comfort or confiding in another caring person is usually banished by severe threats against ever revealing what happened.

Therefore, most severely abused children have no other option than to dissociate those feelings away from their conscious awareness and to carry them unresolved into their adult lives. In DID the unacceptable emotions may be relegated to certain alters who have limited interaction with the external world.

Wherever they are hidden, those sequestered emotions never disappear permanently. While they may appear to lie completely dormant, their energy is often diverted into physical channels, causing a variety of psychosomatic ailments. In most cases those seemingly benign emotions will eventually re-appear. Because of the many intervening years, however, their true source may not be readily evident.

Their Manner of Expression

When a survivor has repressed or dissociated her childhood emotions, she will generally exhibit one of several emotional patterns as an adult. At one extreme, she may appear to be unusually devoid of emotions, not only in speaking of her abuse but in responding to current situations as well. This is generally because she is still living under the deep childhood conviction that emotions are unacceptable. For the sake of safety she has continued to repress her naturally occurring emotions or to divert them into other alters, which enables her to appear totally placid on the surface.

At the other extreme, a survivor may experience sporadic episodes of intense, seemingly inappropriate emotions, which may cause significant problems in her life and personal relationships. While this often results in much blame being cast on her, these seemingly unnatural outbursts are quite explainable. She has just reached the point at which the dissociative barriers separating her from her long-buried emotions are weakening. Therefore, whenever an incident occurs that is in the least bit reminiscent of an unresolved event of the past, it opens the door to the buried emotions from the past, allowing them to release some of their pent-up energy as well. The result is that the person erupts with a volcano of emotions to a seemingly minor offense.

This can be very confusing to both the survivor and those around her. Not only can it damage relationships which are important to the survivor, but it can also cause her to feel a lot of guilt and self-condemnation. She often can't understand why she can't control her emotions like she used to be able to do so well.

Once the survivor is able to understand the dynamic that is occurring at these times, she can use them as opportunities to gain a greater understanding of her buried emotional "garbage." She can also learn to "catch" herself and make a deliberate effort to re-direct the force of her reactions onto the past atrocities instead of the current irritants. This usually makes life significantly better for those around her and lessens her own inner feelings of guilt as well.

Lying between these two extremes is a third possible pattern which survivors may experience. In that case they live almost constantly with what I call "whispering ghosts" of their buried emotions. They may have a nebulous cloud of gloom engulfing them most of the time or have a tendency to cry easily or for no apparent reason. Others may demonstrate an almost constant irritability or edginess. In most cases, however, the survivor is totally unaware that these niggling emotions are seeping into her consciousness from the huge storehouse of memories and emotions she has dissociated from her conscious awareness.

Whatever pattern a survivor manifests, she will almost always fall victim to the phenomenon of transference as well. This is another subtle and confusing way in which repressed emotions sneak out from their buried crypts.

Webster defines "transference" as "the redirection of feelings and desires . . . unconsciously retained from childhood toward a new object," such as a therapist or a spouse.[1] In other words, some of the difficulties the survivor has in these current relationships may reflect unresolved issues she carries from important relationships in her childhood. Because this occurs on an unconscious level, she genuinely perceives the problem to lie totally in the current situation, when she is, in fact, transferring her patterns of feeling about, acting towards, or responding to a particular problem figure from her childhood onto the "offensive" contemporary. While some point of similarity between the past and present usually exists, thereby triggering the transference, the survivor's reaction is usually blown way out of proportion to reality.

For instance, if a survivor feels utter condemnation when her husband disagrees with her or total rejection when her therapist establishes a boundary in their relationship, she is probably transferring the context of past incidents, when these responses were legitimate, onto the present situation. Because she felt so condemned or rejected by a significant person in her childhood, she unconsciously attaches these same intense feelings to the somewhat similar actions of individuals in her current life.

Transference can also occur when a survivor unconsciously expects a spouse or a support person to satisfy all of her unfulfilled parental longings as a child. When that individual fails to live up to these fantasized expectations, the survivor may express emotions which reflect her feelings concerning the failures of her real parents.

Understanding the dynamics of transference is extremely important for anyone functioning as a support person to an abuse survivor, as you can certainly expect some kind of transference to occur within the relationship. Therefore, whenever you can't logically understand a survivor's actions or reactions to you, consider this possibility. She may be unconsciously responding as if you were her childhood perpetrator, her non-protecting parent, or the idealized parent she never had.

Once the transference dynamic is recognized, it gives the problem a whole new perspective. Not only may it clarify what is occurring, but it can also provide a handle for addressing the pertinent childhood issue within the survivor from which it arises. Be prepared, however, for the possibility that the survivor may not recognize or accept the link between the past and the present as quickly as you do. Even if she is reluctant to acknowledge it, however, *your* increased insight will perhaps enable you to respond to her with greater patience and understanding while maintaining your own healthy boundaries with her.

Another important dynamic to be aware of when transference occurs in a relationship is the possibility that you could respond to it in a way that reflects your own unresolved issues from the past. This is called "counter-transference." When your unresolved emotional issues get entangled with the survivor's, you can be of no help to her. The healthiest option in such a case is to withdraw from each other while you both address your own issues. Ask God to help you make this separation in a sensitive manner.

Their Appropriateness

Because of the powerful messages and conditioning that abuse survivors received as children, they are generally quite confused about the appropriateness of their emotions. Being shamed or punished for showing an emotional response to abuse implants a message deep within a child's mind that such emotions are unacceptable.

Children groomed to participate in rituals or the production of child pornography are often deliberately conditioned to reflect no emotional reaction at all, regardless of what they experience. Such children are taught that control over their emotions is a virtue or an indicator of strength. Once established, these false beliefs will be carried into adulthood and continue to hinder the survivor's emotional health. They need to be traced back to the memories in which they originated and specifically countered with truth.

Those who believe that they are not supposed to have emotions need to learn that emotions are a normal and healthy part of everyone's life. If they were scolded or punished for their emotions, they need to learn that emotions are completely amoral. They can never be judged as good or bad, right or wrong. Sometimes what people choose to *do* with their emotions can be wrong but not the feelings themselves. Emotions are natural human responses to life's events. Their existence is as normal and as uncontrollable as hiccups, yawns, and sneezes.

Survivors who were taught that stifling emotions is the strong, mature way to handle them need to learn that emotions represent powerful energy. If that energy is not released in a healthy manner, it will affect the person in many indirect ways. In addition to causing psychosomatic physical ailments, repressed emotional energy can lead to depression, irritability, and other mental and emotional effects.

Learning truth on a cognitive level is rarely sufficient to change beliefs established in terrifying situations. As I explain in the next section, those beliefs must be addressed in the emotional context in which they were acquired.

Even after the belief is changed at this deep level, the survivor may struggle with breaking the old behavior patterns. She will have to overcome the tremendous fear that has been attached for so long to the issue of expressing emotions. Success will come only as she repeatedly dares to do so and experiences no adverse effects.

As a supporter, you can play an important role in this process by encouraging her in the right direction whenever you sense her stifling or otherwise struggling with the validity of her emotions. Repeatedly giving her permission to feel, own, and verbalize her emotions and then validating whatever emotions she does express will help her feel that her emotions really are legitimate. The more she hears and experiences your permission and validation, the more bold and successful she will be in overcoming her unhealthy patterns.

The following is an excellent example of how a therapist responded to his client's reluctance to allow the expression of what she called "stupid, blubbery emotions" belonging to some of her child alters who had just revealed some very traumatic memories:

> Do you want a reason for their blubbering and being all upset? You've been terribly, terribly hurt and you weren't allowed to react to it. You had terrible things done to you—terrible pain done to you—and yet in the midst of it you had to be controlled, you had to be perfect, you had to be still, and you had to do something with all the scared and hurt feelings, didn't you? You had to put those feelings away, and now you have this big pool of feeling, a big pool of hurt. . . from years and years of having to be stuffed down, stuffed down, stuffed down, don't feel, don't feel, don't feel. . . . Do you think that the little girl that had that electrode stuck on her chest and was shocked didn't hurt like mad? She deserves to know that her feelings are being validated by us too. She hurt terribly. It was scary. It was frightening. It was confusing. . . . Yet you knew that

> if you reacted back then, it would just make it worse. And you found a way to get through that without expressing any hurt. It doesn't mean that it wasn't there. It's there. It's very real and it's very deep. And that little girl needs to be able to express her hurt. The five year old [male alter] that was urinated on needs to be allowed to express how humiliated he felt. They couldn't cry back then. But it's okay to feel it now. I'm going to be here with you to get through it. Just let it out. You deserve to let it out. It's okay to start to feel the real feelings again.[2]

A therapist, of course, is supposed to be able to handle the full force of a survivor's emotions. Your capacity may not necessarily be as great. Evaluating this up front and establishing your own boundaries is wise. You need to consider your own emotional health and the effect that another's pain or anger might have on your own "unfinished business." Taking care of yourself and not entering a role in which you cannot perform well is the healthiest route for you to take, both for yourself and for the survivor.

Processing Memories

The true goal of therapy is not just for the survivor to learn how to express her emotions, however. Rather, it is to bring healing to the underlying sources of pain. This requires accessing the traumatic memories in which the emotions are rooted and processing those events in a manner which seeks to eliminate the ongoing pain.

While physical pain was a very real part of the original trauma, the predominant ongoing pain is usually emotional in nature and is based on the *message(s)*, or *belief(s)*, which the child carried away from the event. Because children inherently lack mature cognitive skills, they are exceptionally prone to misinterpret what occurred and why. They often blame themselves and judge their worth and value as a person in tremendously inaccurate ways.

Ritual abuse survivors are prone to even more misconceptions as cultists often deliberately use drugs, sensory overload, sleep deprivation, hypnosis, and other illusionary tactics to a distort their perception of reality. Cult perpetrators are keenly aware of the importance of beliefs in shaping behavior. Therefore, they intentionally structure events to manipulate survivors' beliefs in order to instill a sense of utter powerlessness and control by the cult.

Whether ritually abused or not, the end result is that many of the beliefs that children carry away from their traumatic experiences are simply not true. This is unfortunate because of the years of unnecessary pain those false beliefs perpetuate in their lives. The silver lining to this dark cloud, however, is that even though the traumatic events cannot be undone, the memories can be revisited and the erroneous messages they spawned in the child corrected to reflect truth. When this occurs, the pain associated with them is instantly dispelled.

The other encouraging factor is that facilitating this kind of healing does not necessarily require a skilled therapist. Supporters who are willing to learn the basic procedure can often be extremely effective in this kind of ministry. They will also find that it works just as well in bringing healing to painful memories in non-multiples as well.

The steps involved are quite simple but very important for keeping the process on track. Memory work is never pleasant, but by focusing on a specific goal, the intensified pain evoked in the survivor will be not only productive but also confined to a minimum length of time.

The first step is to trace the pain (or other emotion) that the survivor is currently feeling back to its origin. Starting with what the survivor is already in touch with is most efficient because the door to the memory from which it comes is already open. Therefore, you just have to ask her to drift back in her mind to when she first felt this pain, or you can ask Jesus to take her to the memory. If He believes she is ready to encounter it, He may put her instantly in touch with it.

Sometimes neither of these methods will successfully connect the survivor with the originating memory. Unfortunately, the many other dynamics operating in a multiple's life can interfere with the process. Some involve the survivor herself while others were deliberately imposed upon her system by her perpetrators.

Remember that in dissociated individuals the entire system of alter-identities is deeply committed to keeping the Core and Host separated from knowledge of the trauma. Sometimes significant psychological conflicts around the issue of "knowing" need to be resolved before the mind will release the memory. In ritual abuse survivors programming or demonization may be involved in causing the block. While you may be able to remove demonic blocks through spiritual warfare, addressing programming or conflict issues may require a therapist's attention.

When contact with the traumatic memory is successful, however, the next step is to identify the belief(s) underlying the pain (or other troubling symptoms). You can help the survivor pinpoint this by asking questions such as "Why does this hurt so badly?" "Why does this make you so angry?" "What did you come away believing about yourself, others, or life in general?" or "What decisions did you make because this happened?"

Don't bombard her with all of these questions at once. Use your own sensitivity to decide which one would be most applicable in the situation. If your first question doesn't produce a clear belief, try another. Be sure she understands that the beliefs you are searching for must come out of her emotional state at the time of the event, which might be totally different from what her adult mind tells her is true.

While each survivor must identify these messages for herself in each situation, some of the common beliefs which children carry away from abusive events are:

- It was my fault.
- I am bad.
- I am dirty, contaminated.
- I am unlovable.

- I don't matter.
- My body is not my own.
- I am possessed by my perpetrator.
- I am powerless to protect myself.
- I am powerless to change anything.

These beliefs may sound simplistic, but the implications that they carry in the survivor's life are enormous. Usually the beliefs giving rise to the greatest pain focus on the person's identity, worth, or destiny in life.

When the specific message causing the pain is identified, the survivor's anguish will usually increase. While this is uncomfortable, healing is most effective when she is actively embracing the full impact of the believed message as you embark upon the next step, which is to challenge its accuracy.

One powerful way of doing this, if you and the survivor are both comfortable with it, is to invite Jesus to address the truthfulness of the belief. While you must never assume that He will answer "on demand," He will frequently choose to intervene in some way that clearly impresses upon the survivor or alter what the *truth* really is. When this occurs, both the false belief and the pain derived from it instantly evaporate. Peace and calm replace the often gut-wrenching agony previously experienced.[3]

This method for healing emotional pain is based on John 8:32, where Jesus said, "You will know the truth, and the truth will set you free." Because God is the author of all truth, the same measure of healing can result regardless of the means by which the truth is received.

Sometimes in the course of revisiting a memory, the deliberate manipulations of the cult to deceive the survivor will become clear, and recognizing this *truth* will banish her false beliefs based upon it. At other times a particular identity's beliefs about a situation can be totally revolutionized by having another identity supply a piece of *truth* which was previously missing because of the dissociative barriers, and this will instantly dispel the troublesome false belief. Reading carefully chosen portions of Scripture may sometimes be effective in bringing *truth* if they precisely address the specific belief causing the survivor's pain.

While healing truth can be received from any source that the survivor accepts as an authority, be cautious about trying to supply that piece of truth yourself. Jesus is the only One who consistently knows what particular truth the survivor needs in each situation. That is why He is the best one to supply the truth. While the possibility of deception from demons or other alters certainly exists when seeking truth from God, what is not truth will be immediately known because it will fail to have a healing effect on the survivor.

Sometimes the emotional pain being felt by the survivor is connected to a series of memories linked together by a common false belief. Complete healing seemingly requires that she be in touch with the memory of the event at which that belief was *first* established.

Therefore, when Jesus does not respond to your request to bring *truth* or the healing does not seem complete, it may be due to the fact that the survivor is not yet in touch with that critical initial memory. In this case you can ask Jesus to continue leading her back further and further until she reaches it. Recognize again, however, that unresolved conflicts involving a perceived need for denial may have to be addressed first. Therefore, don't continue to force this probe for a deeper memory if it is not readily revealed.

When *truth* is received and the pain is removed from a memory, it may no longer be considered intolerable. This may lead to further healing as the dissociative barriers which have isolated the identities embodying it for so many years may no longer be needed. Bringing truth to a major false belief in one memory may impact many other memories as well if their intolerable nature was based on the same false belief. This can really be exciting and bring significant encouragement to the survivor.

Anger

In addition to pain, abuse also generates anger. While the pain is often augmented by false beliefs, the anger is usually fully justified. It is the body's natural response to a wrong suffered. Because it was usually not safe or permissible for the survivor to express her anger at the time of the abuse, it becomes a significant issue to be addressed in the healing process.

Resolving anger begins in a manner similar to pain in that it needs to be connected to a specific incident or issue. Because of the dissociation and many intervening years, the specific source of the anger is not always obvious to the survivor at first. Nevertheless, the best starting place is to ask her to define whom she is angry at and why.

If she reports that her anger stems from a recent event, but its intensity seems excessive, its extra force is probably coming from a similar, but more serious, incident in her past. You can probe for this deeper source by asking if she remembers feeling this kind of anger before or if she sees anything about the issue inciting her current anger that reminds her of her past abuse.

Once she connects her anger to its true root, she needs to ascertain its validity. Was she truly wronged, or is her anger based on an inaccurate perception of the event? Help her process the memory as described above to rectify any erroneous beliefs associated with it. Anger which was rooted in a false belief will instantly dissolve when the belief is corrected.

If her anger is based on an accurate assessment of the original event and she truly was wronged, she needs a safe way to express her anger so its energy can be dissipated. Several options can provide this necessary release. She can use the Gestalt technique of imagining her perpetrator sitting in a chair in front of her and then vocalizing the full extent of her anger as if to his or her true presence. In the Bible, David sometimes did this (Ps. 53:1-5; 55:12-14). At other times he vehemently expressed his anger directly to God (e.g. Ps. 35:11-25; 69), and the survivor can do this as well if she chooses.

Sometimes engaging in a physical activity while verbalizing one's anger helps to dissipate more of its energy. In this case she can beat a chair cushion with her fist or a tennis racket, or she can whack a counter or the back of a chair with a rolled up newspaper.

These more physical means of releasing anger are especially necessary when the strength of the anger being felt might lead the survivor to some form of violence. Anger of this potency is not unusual in survivors of severe abuse. If the survivor is extremely distraught, she may need to initiate a controlled physical activity even before analyzing the exact nature and source of her anger. You can then help guide her thinking in this direction as she is engaged in it or after its energy is reduced to a more manageable level.

Forgiveness is another key component of dealing with anger, but the relationship between the two dynamics is often confusing. **Anger** is a *feeling*. Therefore, its *existence* is not under the control of the will. It is the body's *natural response* to a wrong suffered. It is not condemned by God unless it is acted out in a harmful way or retained too long (Eph. 4:26).

Hate is often closely associated with anger, perhaps fueled by it. It must not be confused with anger, however. **Hate** is not a feeling; it is a *chosen attitude* which desires revenge or wishes ill on another person.

Forgiveness is an *act of the will* by which we mentally release a perpetrator from his "debt" to us (Luke 11:4 KJV), that is, the penalty which justice demands for his wrongdoing. Through forgiveness we relinquish all demands for retribution and desires for revenge to God and His higher tribunal of justice (Rom. 12:19; Gen. 18:26). **Forgiveness** thus surrenders the hate we carry in our hearts towards our abusers.

By giving God the responsibility for bringing justice, a survivor can regain emotional health in spite of being grievously wronged. When viewed in this light, forgiveness is truly a gift from God! If she rejects this gift, hate and bitterness will become destructive forces in her life, affecting her physically, emotionally, socially, and spiritually. She will also remain emotionally chained to her perpetrator(s) and his/her offenses. Withholding forgiveness actually gives her perpetrator(s) the power to continue to damage her life.

Many people believe that forgiveness should automatically eliminate one's anger towards the offender. They fail to recognize that anger is a natural emotion and thus cannot be affected by an act of the will.

Often they are also confusing anger and hate. Hate is a chosen attitude of desiring revenge on one's perpetrator. This hate, and whatever anger was associated with it, will indeed be gone when true forgiveness is granted. However, anger related to other aspects of the offense may linger.

Anger in its purest form says, "I don't like this!" It doesn't say, "I hate you!" That is a decision that can, and often does, grow out of anger, but it is not inherent in it. When we forgive someone, we remove this appendage to our anger—and usually a huge part of the anger also dissolves. It is possible, however, that some of the "I don't like this!" remains. In a sense forgiveness is saying, "In spite of how I *feel* about this, I am *choosing* not to have an attitude of revenge against the offender. I can still say, however, "I don't like this and this and this about what I am going through!" and say it with varying degrees of intensity.

The survivor must fully understand this so that she will address any remaining anger in a healthy manner and not try to deny its existence by repressing it or turning it inward on herself again. Such anger is especially understandable when memories are fresh or still emerging.

Holding onto any form of lingering anger, resentment, or self-pity legitimate anger for any significant length of time will be detrimental to the survivor's health physically, emotionally, and spiritually, however. Therefore, she must continue to process the offense and seek inner healing from its effects so she can put it to rest. If the anger is particularly strong, she may need to ventilate it in a more physical way so its energy gets depleted.

The complicating dynamics of DID must also be kept in mind when addressing the survivor's anger. As long as dissociation is in place, the alters must be recognized as each having a separate part of the survivor's mind, will, and emotions. Therefore, just because one part has resolved its anger and forgiveness issues does not mean that they all have.

You should also expect anger, hate, and forgiveness to wax and wane throughout the therapeutic journey as new memories and issues continue to arise. Forgiveness is not necessarily a "once and for all" thing. Each wave of new awareness of the brutality the survivor suffered will naturally be accompanied by anger and perhaps hate as well. Therefore, whenever the survivor recognizes that she is directing thoughts of ill will towards her perpetrator(s), she must again relinquish this to God if she is to experience the emotional freedom that He desires for her.

Guilt

One of the common lies that child abuse victims believe is that whatever happened to them was their fault. Sometimes perpetrators deliberately impress this upon them, but often they come to this conclusion on their own. The guilt they feel often contributes to a desire to lock the memories away in their minds and neither look at them nor talk about them.

Whether guilt is openly expressed or hidden in the back of their minds, it needs to be addressed. This again means identifying the *beliefs* that makes them feel guilty. The truth of these beliefs must then be challenged as discussed above. Usually when truth replaces the false beliefs survivors are carrying concerning guilt, they experience a tremendous inner relief, which is often accompanied by a significant lifting of their spirits.

With ritual abuse survivors the feelings of guilt can be even more pronounced as they were generally not only incredibly traumatized themselves but also forced to traumatize others. If their cult involvement was extensive, they probably even participated in human sacrifices and other criminal acts. Furthermore, if they had younger siblings or even children of their own who were under the age of seven and able to dissociate, their cult-involved alters may have been forced to bring them into cult activities as well.

All such acts of perpetration were usually totally contrary to both the will and the moral standards of the Core. They could only be tolerated through extreme dissociation. Therefore, the protective walls concealing these memories will be exceptionally strong. Sooner or later, however, in order for healing to be complete, the survivor will have to face and own these seemingly unbearable realities.

As these memories come into her consciousness, she may be overcome by intense feelings of guilt. When those victimized by her actions were her own siblings or children, she may feel totally incapable of handling the implications. Her vehement self-blame may potentially lead her to serious acts of self-punishment or suicide.

This is an extremely critical time for the survivor to have the support of other caring individuals who can understand and affirm her emotions but also provide objectivity. The main goal in addressing her enormous feelings of guilt is to help her discern where true responsibility for evil acts lies. She is *not* responsible for actions she was forced—or manipulated—into performing. The one *forcing* the action bears the guilt (Mark 9:42). Often Jesus is the only one who can truly convince the survivor of this. He told one survivor who had participated in a ritual sacrifice that she was "as innocent as the knife."

This is the truth every survivor with this kind of history must grasp. They were used and had absolutely no choice in the matter. Their alter-identities were exploited and maneuvered by intense, terror-filled double binds to perform as virtual robots.

Sometimes perpetrator acts were deliberately forced upon the survivor for the sole purpose of creating such intense feelings of guilt that her psyche would respond by isolating the event behind a strong dissociative barrier, which would not only protect the Core and Host from knowledge of the event but also effectively hide the activities the cultists desired to keep secret. At other times perpetrators may have forced an alter to commit a crime just so they could use it as blackmail to secure the alter's silence by threatening, "If you tell what *we* did, we'll tell what *you* did—and you'll go to jail!"

Fear

By far the most powerful emotion used for manipulation by perpetrators, however, is fear. Any kind of abuse is frightening in itself, but many perpetrators threaten their victims with even more fearsome consequences if they should fail to cooperate or should ever talk about what happened.

Fear is the driving force behind all the mechanisms of control used within cults, including programming. Cult victims were repeatedly subjected to terrifying and life-threatening double binds in which the only way out was to comply with the wishes of the perpetrators. Through this means cultists could essentially force survivors into any desired behavioral response.

Whatever the source of the abuse, survivors are left with extensive ongoing fears. In fact, whenever they encounter anything that was previously associated with their terrifying abuse experiences, their subconscious minds automatically associate it with those previous events, and they instantly respond with the same adrenaline-pumping fear. They may not even be consciously aware of the specific memories in which the triggers are rooted, but their emotions respond just the same.

Virtually anything associated with their perpetrators, the cult, or their abuse, whether deliberately used or randomly present, can trigger flashback reactions of fear and panic when encountered at a later time. These triggers may include specific types of animals, birds, insects, objects, symbols, colors, odors, etc.. They can be activities associated with the abuse or the cult, such as sitting in circles or around bonfires, chanting, or swaying to music. They may be various locations in which the abuse took place, such as woods, barns, mines, or caves. Even weather conditions which occurred during the abuse or behaviors which evoked strong punishment, such as saying, "No," doing something "wrong," or performing imperfectly, can strike a chord of terror within survivors. Encountering any of these triggers frequently provokes a switch, often to the victim alter most directly related to the fear or a protector alter who believes the survivor is in imminent danger.

Understanding why these fears exist and why they are so powerful, so tenacious, and often so seemingly irrational is critical to the role of a support person. Discounting them or expecting them to be quickly resolved will be counterproductive. As you learn the particular things which trigger the survivor you are supporting, you can be alert for them and, when possible, even protect her from unnecessary exposure to what may cause an uncomfortable reaction in her.

Because these fears are generally associated with survival threatening situations, they are extremely difficult to erase. If the memories in which they are rooted have not yet surfaced, working on overcoming the fears is virtually impossible. Even after the memories arise, desensitizing the triggers may take time. You may choose to be less protective in guarding the survivor from exposure to them, but consult with her therapist before deliberately confronting her with a known trigger for the purpose of desensitization.

When a survivor does encounter a trigger and her fears erupt, treat her with gentleness, patience, comfort, and reassurance. Help her notice the differences between the current setting and the past terror-evoking events, especially the things which may indicate her safety in the present situation.

Keep in mind, too, that fears can sometimes be demonically driven, in which case spiritual warfare is the proper antidote. Fear in itself can also be a foothold which empowers demonic activity. Therefore, encouraging the survivor to deal with her fears is important. It can never be forced, however. She must be personally motivated and willing to cooperate in the effort.

Processing Current Life Experiences

In addition to processing traumatic events from the past, survivors often need to talk about things that are transpiring in their current lives. The dynamics of dissociation and programming (when present), as well as the emotionally upsetting nature of the therapy process, make everyday life a little more complicated and challenging for multiples. Emotions and frustrations often mount and need a chance to be ventilated. You can be a great help by lending a listening ear, providing an objective perspective, and at times offering some good advice.

The survivor's inter-personal relationships is a subject often needing such dialog. Her relationship with her family of origin may involve particularly complex dynamics. To what extent they believe and support her can vary greatly and have an immense impact on her. If they happen to be her perpetrators, these relationships carry a multitude of potent, and often conflicting, emotions. Ongoing or sporadic contact with *any* former perpetrator can be extremely upsetting. These are all situations in which the survivor needs a listening ear as well as wise and compassionate support.

If the survivor also has a family acquired through marriage, these relationships are majorly affected by her abuse issues as well. She may carry a tremendous amount of grief over the difficulties she knows she causes for those she loves the most. If she is able to work, that is another setting where special challenges may occur. Being able to talk to another caring individual about these things can be very helpful and also enables therapy time to focus on issues that really do require a therapist.

One of the key elements which talking to another person provides is perspective. Because a multiple's life experience and memory are divided through dissociation, perspective often gets distorted. If alter-identities lack a complete picture of a given situation, they can easily jump to wrong conclusions and go through unnecessary emotional reactions. Sometimes another person with a more objective perspective can turn a mountain into a mole hill rather quickly.

This isn't always true, however. Sometimes an alter can be extremely convinced that her perspective is absolutely right! In these cases the combined input of several other people agreeing on a particular point of view may be necessary to convince her that she isn't seeing the whole picture.

Survivors also need help with perspective in recognizing when they overreact to things in the present because of their unresolved issues from the past. Whether buried anger is "piggy-backing" on a current situation or transference is distorting a relationship, survivors often have a difficult time recognizing when these dynamics occur. Therefore, an objective and supportive person can not only be instrumental in providing this perspective but also help the survivor identify and process the root issues creating the problem.

The presence of demonic activity in their lives is another time survivors may need help with perspective. Satan may work to amplify a survivor's sense of guilt, shame, or defilement in an effort to undermine her self-worth as well as her perception of acceptance by God or worthiness of His forgiveness. These lies could potentially drive her to hopelessness, despair, or even suicide.

When completely overwhelmed by negative thoughts and emotions, survivors may never consider the possibility of demons implanting these thoughts or augmenting their emotions. If you can keep the potential of Satanic involvement in mind at these times and gently suggest this when you feel it is appropriate, you can often significantly limit the survivor's misery. An immediate change in her mental or emotional state after addressing the issue through spiritual warfare will indicate that Satan was indeed involved.

Endnotes

[1] *Merriam-Webster's Collegiate Dictionary*, 10th ed. (1993), s.v. "transference."

[2] David Witkovsky, therapy session, 1997.

[3] Ed Smith of Campbellsville, KY, coined the term "Theophostic" (God + Light) to describe this approach to emotional healing. Restoration in Christ Ministries call their adaptation of these principles "Truth Ministry."

Chapter Seven

Protective Support

Protective support involves helping to ensure the physical safety of abuse survivors in crisis situations. Unfortunately, self-harm and suicidal tendencies are quite common among this particular population. When the person is in danger of acting upon these, the situation requires immediate intervention.

Suicidal Ideation

Intense emotions, extreme loneliness, or overwhelming despair can often move an abuse survivor to think of suicide. In ritual abuse, external dynamics are often used to drive the survivor to suicide at certain times as well.

Cult perpetrators usually use some form of mind control programming to keep their subjects under their control and serving their purposes. This sophisticated form of conditioning places a child in a terrifying double bind in which the desired response is seen as the only way out. By repeatedly attaching a specific "trigger" to this event, encountering the trigger alone will eventually compel the same response. Through this mechanism, perpetrators can compel an almost automatic response of self-harm or suicide if strictly prohibited behaviors occur, such as any breach of secrecy or disobedience to major cult directives.

Sacrifice of oneself to Satan or some other supposed deity is often expected in Satanic cults. Even unwilling alters can be manipulated into making such vows under extreme duress. Often a specific date is set, perhaps decades in advance, and programming put in place to ensure the carrying out of this commitment.

Personal experience also indicates that demons may view being expelled from a person without accomplishing their assignments as demoralizing. Therefore, if deliverance seems imminent or progress in therapy in any way threatens the success of their mission, they may attempt to drive the survivor to commit suicide. From their perspective the survivor's suicide will spare them the horrible disgrace of being expelled in complete failure. While a demon cannot superimpose its will over the will of a Christian survivor, it is capable of injecting compulsive, morbid thoughts and/or inflicting tremendous psychic torment within the survivor's mind, which can sometimes impel the drastic response they desire.

Since demonic torment is an excellent way to enhance compliance, cult-involved alters are frequently manipulated to establish a legal ground for demonic attachments. These demons can seemingly be given specific assignments that serve to enhance programming or ensure that the vows, oaths, and commitments the person made in the cult are indeed fulfilled, including those involving self sacrifice.

If the survivor you are supporting becomes suicidal, you must quickly ascertain how serious she is. If you find her in a situation in which she has already jeopardized her life or is in the midst of doing so, you, of course, need to get her immediate help from the proper medical/mental health authorities.

If she is talking about ending her life but has not yet taken steps to do so, you have a couple options. While it is always appropriate to call her therapist, if you have a significant relationship with her and feel able to address her system in a knowledgeable manner, you can try a few things yourself to resolve the situation.

While any threat of suicide needs to be taken seriously, the unique dynamics of DID must also kept in mind. Rarely does the whole system want to die. Therefore, the two main questions to ask are: "Who wants to die?" and "Why?"

If an alter wants to die, other identities who are highly committed to life can often counterbalance the drive for death. Furthermore, the issue driving an alter's desire to die, when identified, can often be quickly resolved. Frequently the alter does not have a complete or accurate picture of reality. If this is the case, you can try to correct that picture. This may require insight that you yourself can supply or that the Host or another part of the system can supply or that you can quickly find out from another person. If this resolves the situation, the crisis is over.

If a primary identity, such as the Core and/or Host, wants to die, the situation is more critical as the alter-identities may not have sufficient ego strength to overpower her. Therefore, you must identify and challenge the underlying *belief* driving the desire for death. Often bringing truth to this belief will dispel the desire for death.

If, for whatever reason, you cannot successfully resolve the issue yourself, you need to change your focus to keeping the survivor safe until her therapist can work with her to do this. If you can find parts of the system that do not want to die, try to get one of them to come out and stay in control of the body while you make arrangements to get the survivor the help she needs. However, do not leave her alone.

Call her primary therapist and see how soon he or she can meet with her. Together you can then decide whether you feel you can keep her safe and under constant surveillance until that time or whether you need to take her to a hospital. This will depend on her state of agitation or despondency as well as your resources of time and a place for setting up a vigil.

Self-Harm

Self-harm can be a significant issue for any abuse survivor, but it is particularly common among ritual abuse survivors. It can take many forms, including cutting, clawing, burning, bruising, and even fracturing bones of the body. The mechanisms driving this behavior can be quite complex.

Sometimes purely human strategies are involved. Alter-identities known as "persecutors" may use self-harm to punish other alters whom they believe are not performing properly. These alters either were manipulated and brainwashed to take on the agenda of the perpetrators or surmised very quickly that identifying with them was the safest route to go. Therefore, they virtually serve as internal representatives of the abuser(s) and instigate punishment whenever they perceive another identity's plans or actions to be displeasing to the external abuser(s).

As strange as it may sound, some protector alters may also cut or hurt the body when they feel the person is misperforming in the eyes of the perpetrator(s). In this case they are trying to warn the person that they are in danger of much more serious repercussions from the perpetrator(s) if they do not amend their ways. Only a multiple can understand how effectively dissociation enables an alter to view the body that gets hurt as not being her own.

For other alters, self-harm serves as a silent release for powerful emotions which they believe can be discharged in no other way or a way not to feel so utterly powerless in an overwhelming situation. Still others use it as a coping strategy, endeavoring to convert intense emotional pain into physical pain, which to them seems more bearable, or to cause an adrenaline release that will bring a change in mental state.

Some clinicians believe that subjecting the body to trauma is a means of strengthening the dissociative walls which protect the Core and the Host from knowing the intolerable realities of their abuse. Therefore, if something occurs which threatens this desired separation, some part of the system may deliberately subject the body to trauma in an effort to strengthen the dissociative barriers between the Core and Host and the trauma-bearing parts of the system.

This may occur, for example, if overwhelming memories surface, endangering secrets are revealed, incriminating evidence is discovered, or a past perpetrator re-enters the survivor's life. Because of this possibility whenever self-harm occurs, exploring whether the system is feeling a new threat of some kind is a wise step. Often addressing this issue will defuse the perceived need for further harm.

For ritual abuse survivors, self-injury can be connected to programming or demonization. In the Bible the demonized man of the Gadarenes is described as cutting himself with stones (Mark 5:5). Sometimes a demonized person or alter will give in to a demon's pressure to injure the body just to get the torment to stop or to provide an alternate focus of attention.

Often demons work in conjunction with persecutor or controller alters to inflict physical punishment on disobedient alters. Demons might also try to harm the body to strike back or to relieve their own torment when spiritual warfare is being conducted and they can't leave because the legal ground for their attachment has not been renounced. Therefore, if self-harm is being inflicted during spiritual warfare, stop and determine why it is happening. Command that all that is demonic be separated from that which is human while the search for legal grounds or other pertinent ties is pursued.

In other situations if you are with a survivor when she attempts to harm herself, trying to restrain her physically is appropriate. However, use as little force as is necessary and try not to exhibit anger. You do not want to jeopardize the trust of the system or further enflame the situation.

As soon as possible try to find out who in the system is doing or wanting to do the self-harm and why. By drawing out and validating the feelings of this part, you open the door for verbal ventilation, which can significantly reduce the force driving the desire for self-injury. If the alter is extremely distraught, suggest a safer way to let out some of the energy behind her feelings, such as pounding on a pillow or hitting a counter with a rolled up newspaper.

You can also do spiritual warfare in case the situation is being demonically driven. However, if the survivor has not acknowledged the possible influence of demons, rebuke them as quietly as possible or ask God to deal with them. If an alter is responsible for the self-harm, she is apt to be further enraged to have you attribute her actions to demons.

Sometimes helping the alter identify possible distortions in her perspective or asking Jesus to address the accuracy of the belief which is driving the self-harm can end the crisis. If not, you will have to phone her therapist and follow the instructions given in the previous section to provide safety for the survivor.

Pros and Cons of Hospitalization

When the issues driving self-harm or a desire for suicide ideation cannot be quickly resolved, survivors may need around-the-clock surveillance to ensure their safety until whatever is precipitating the crisis can be resolved. Hospitalization is sometimes an option for providing this. However, the survivor must have insurance—or significant financial resources.

Another potential problem is that many psychiatric hospitals refuse to recognize the reality of DID and/or ritual abuse. Treatment in such a hospital would not be in the survivor's best interests and might even feel abusive. It could also set her therapy back. Specialized in-patient DID units do exist in scattered hospitals around the United States, but rarely do they have clinical staff trained to address both the psychological and spiritual dynamics which occur with ritual abuse survivors. The bottom line, however, is that any psychiatric hospital or ward is usually able to keep a survivor safe if no other options exist.

In lieu of hospitalization the survivor may occasionally need a team of volunteers working in rotating shifts to provide the necessary surveillance to keep her safe. These people must be capable of physically, but non-abusively, restraining the survivor when necessary. Also, the more familiar they are with the dynamics of DID, conflict resolution, spiritual warfare, and the alter system of the survivor, the better equipped they will be to work with the survivor in a manner which diminishes, rather than enhances, the dynamics driving the crisis.

Sometimes a similar period of "constant companionship" may be needed to protect the survivor from physical access by the cult as well, particularly around significant Satanic holidays (see Appendix C). In either situation be careful in choosing the location for such heightened surveillance so that small children are not exposed to potential violence or demonic confrontation. The need for this degree of physical protection varies greatly from survivor to survivor—and from month-to-month, week-to-week, or even day-to-day—in any given survivor.

Chapter Eight

Spiritual Support

Abuse survivors frequently have distorted images of God and of their relationship to Him. They need these misperceptions to be brought in line with truth and to learn to walk in the fullness of their spiritual heritage through Jesus Christ. Some may need to find Christ as their personal Savior and to learn how to draw upon His divine resources in their daily lives. Therefore, helping a survivor grow spiritually is another valuable area of support you can offer.

Ritual abuse survivors have an even greater need for spiritual support as they are deliberately held in bondage by spiritual forces of evil in addition to the deep psychological issues arising from their severe trauma. They will never achieve complete healing through human resources alone. God is the only One having the power and authority to overcome the forces of Satan ensnaring their souls—and He will do it in response to the prayers and spiritual warfare of His people.

Prayer

While spiritual support may involve other aspects as well, prayer will always be a primary focus. Prayer unlocks the door to the outpouring of God's power, wisdom, and guidance for you, the survivor, and her therapist. It is not only vital in achieving her healing but is crucial for addressing your inadequacies as well. While you may frequently feel at a complete loss in knowing how to help the survivor, God perfectly understands the issues and dynamics operating in her life. He also has the power to intervene, either acting directly in the survivor's life or guiding you in meeting the need. Your weakness is merely an opportunity for God to release His resources in you (2 Cor. 3:4-5; 12:9-10).

The powerful resource of prayer can be implemented without necessarily having direct contact with the survivor if that is inconvenient or uncomfortable. However, you obviously can pray most knowledgeably when you have some means of staying current with specific and ongoing needs. If several individuals are involved in providing spiritual support for a survivor, a prayer chain solely for this purpose can be an effective way to convey requests in a timely manner. Of course, confidentiality is always of utmost importance.

Some of the general needs for which survivors of ritual and other forms of abuse need prayer include:

- Adequate finances for therapy and daily living needs;
- Adequate support for them and their families;
- Spiritual protection for themselves, their families, and those helping them.

In regard to their therapy you can pray for:

- Adequate strength, motivation, and courage to face and own the truth;
- Guidance for the therapist,
- Success in identifying and correcting false beliefs,
- Success in identifying and eliminating demonic footholds,
- Success in disarming any programming,
- Discernment of truth from deception wherever Satan is involved.

If a good communication system is established with the survivor, you can pray much more specifically regarding goals for each therapy session. If you can be present in the session, this is even better.

Even if you don't know exactly how to pray for a survivor in a particular situation, you can just lift her name to God and allow the Holy Spirit to intercede on her behalf with "groans that words cannot express" (Rom. 8:26). How awesome it is to know that God's response does not depend on our ability to articulate the right words!

Spiritual Warfare

Because of the extensive demonization that occurs in ritual abuse, anyone providing support for this kind of survivor needs a good grasp of the principles of spiritual warfare and the ability to engage effectively in it. Some may be particularly gifted in assisting in this manner and can play an invaluable role in helping the survivor gain lasting freedom from the forces of darkness she was usually forced to receive against her will. Others can assist in at least binding demons which attempt to interfere with her day-to-day life until they can be dealt with permanently.

You must not enter this role without adequate preparation, however. Satan's forces can easily overpower an unprotected human, especially if you start "stepping on their toes." As a Christian, you may not be physically assaulted like the seven sons of Sceva were in the days of the Apostles (Acts 19:13-16), but you could suffer other significant blows to your well-being. Satan has the ability to manipulate circumstances around you, attack your health, or subtly work to cause moral deterioration in your life (cf. Job; Luke 13:11; 2 Cor. 11:3; 1 Tim. 4:1). This should not be threatening to a mature Christian, however, because God is infinitely more powerful than Satan (1 John 4:4), and He has provided all we need to be completely protected from his crafty schemes (Eph. 6:10-13).

Because Satan is a *spiritual* being and the battle we wage against him occurs on a *spiritual* plane, we need *spiritual* armor as our protection. In Ephesians 6:14-17, God clearly explains the characteristics that comprise our spiritual armor. "Putting it on" must never be viewed as merely a daily ritual of verbally rehearsing the words of these verses. While such a daily reminder is helpful, what provides protection in the spiritual realm is *the manifestation of a lifestyle which consistently exhibits these qualities*. Because this protective armor is so important, the last chapter in this book is devoted to explaining it in greater depth.

Equipping ourselves in this spiritual armor provides our *defense* in the spiritual battle and is totally *our* responsibility. To launch an *offensive* attack against the enemy, we must be equally well prepared, but in this case we must not rely on any resource of our own. Only the power and authority of God Himself can successfully defeat the powers of darkness, and we must never forget this.

God, however, graciously allows His redeemed children to share the same spiritual position of authority in the heavens that He gave to His own Son, Jesus Christ, far above all the ranks of Satan's forces (Eph. 1:20-22; 2:6). Jesus Christ rightly deserves this position through His own divine merit. We share it only through His grace. Therefore, while we can command the obedience of Satan's forces just like Jesus modeled for us during His time on earth, we must do it in the power and authority of *His* name and on the basis of *His* shed blood (Luke 10:17).

If you are not a true child of God through faith in Jesus' death on the Cross for the forgiveness of your sins (John 3:16-18), you do not share His position of authority and can wield no power against Satan or any of his demons. To try to do so could be disastrous (see Acts 19:13-16). When you truly are God's child, however, you can confidently engage in spiritual warfare on behalf of yourself and others, including the survivor(s) you are supporting.

Launching an offensive attack against the spiritual realm of darkness involves authoritatively commanding demons *"in the name of Jesus"* to do exactly what you want or do not want them to do. Because Satanic cultists often deceptively give alters the names of "Jesus" or "God" or try to attach demons by these names to parts of the survivor's alter-identity system, using a more specific description which refers *only* to the *divine* Jesus is often helpful when working with SRA survivors. By using designations such as "Jesus of Nazareth," "the risen Lord Jesus Christ," or "Jesus, my Redeemer," you eliminate all opportunities for confusion and substitution within the system dynamics of the survivor and the spiritual realm.

Usually demons will respond immediately to commands made in Jesus' name. If they do not, you need to consider several potentially complicating factors. Always remember that demons operate very legalistically within a strict authority structure (Eph. 1:21; 6:12). In some situations you may need to address the spiritual beings in higher authority over the one whose activity you are targeting. Jude 8-9 seems to indicate that when dealing with the highest levels of spiritual beings, we need to call upon the Lord to rebuke them rather than do so ourselves. Therefore, when you are not seeing the results you expect, ask God to come against and rebuke all the evil "celestial beings" and spiritual authorities in the heavenlies that are having any influence on the survivor. Some people do this routinely before attempting any other forms of spiritual warfare.

If you notice no effect after making this specific request of God, assume that you are dealing with demons of lesser rank. Demons can employ a lot of stall tactics, but they must ultimately obey. Therefore, be persistent in your efforts, and remember that a demon's response does not depend on the tone or volume of your voice but on the *authority* of name of the Lord Jesus Christ. Therefore, you do not need to get hyped up emotionally to make a demon obey. These fleshly tactics have no effect in the spiritual realm except to amuse and flatter the demons involved.

Instead, rely wholly on spiritual weapons in your offensive attack (2 Cor. 10:3-4). For instance, you can often "turn up the heat" on the enemy by reading from the Bible, speaking, or singing about the shed blood of Jesus through which He triumphed over Satan and his forces (Heb. 2:14; Col. 2:15). These powerful spiritual weapons seem to cause such torment to the demons that they will often comply immediately in order to make it stop. If they do not, however, don't prolong this tactic too long because the person or alter to whom the demon(s) is attached feels the nearly unbearable torment as well.

Another factor to keep in mind is that demons do not have to leave if their presence is based on a legal foothold established in the person's life. In SRA this could be a sacrifice, vow, or covenant which a particular alter made or an evil activity in which she was forced to participate. Sometimes alters willingly receive demons because of the supernatural power they seemingly offer, thinking they will serve to protect them from further trauma. For this reason some alters may also be reluctant to let go of them. Until these footholds are renounced by the specific alter(s) involved, the demon(s) will not have to leave.

You can, however, still use the authority of Jesus to bind their activity (Mat. 16:19). Experience has shown, in fact, that you can be very specific in doing this, even commanding that they be made deaf, dumb, blind, and/or totally paralyzed. You can also at least temporarily cancel their assignments in the individual. When expelling them, you can also command demons not to harm the survivor in any way as they leave. This eliminates all the "theatrics" sometimes experienced in deliverance sessions.

Sometimes in order to work effectively with the alter involved, you need to command the demon(s) to be separated from the human alter. This gives the alter the opportunity to think for herself in deciding whether to break the ties she has to the demon(s).

Some of the areas in which spiritual warfare is particularly needed for ritual abuse survivors include:

- Removing spiritual blindness from the hearts and minds of alters who are in bondage to Satan;
- Prohibiting demons from blocking truth or interfering with therapy;
- Stopping demonically driven fear, anxiety, confusion, torment, or self-harm;
- Stopping demonic communication between the survivor and other cult members;

- Providing spiritual protection;
    - Whenever contact with cult-involved family members is necessary or possible
    - During Satanic holidays when accessing is likely (see Appendix C for calendar dates).

Some examples for addressing these issues are:

- In the name of Jesus Christ, my Redeemer, I bind the ability of all demons to hinder truth and healing in the therapy session today.
- In the name of Jesus Christ of Nazareth I command the demons that are tormenting (name) to stop. Your assignment is cancelled, and you must obey the orders of the risen Lord Jesus Christ instead.
- If demons are in any way contributing to the confusion [name] is feeling, I command in the name of Jesus Christ, the Son of the true Creator God, that you stop and that you become mute and paralyzed.

In praying for spiritual protection, you might pray along these lines:

- Lord Jesus, I ask that You surround [name] with Your holy angels as she travels to her grandmother's. I ask that you block all demonic communication which might emanate from her grandmother or any other cult person associated with her. Allow no physical, emotional, or spiritual harm to come to her.
- Heavenly Father, I pray in the name of Jesus Christ, my risen Redeemer, that You send Your angelic forces in sufficient strength and number to completely overpower all of Satan's forces which may attempt to interfere with the deliverance session scheduled for [name] today.
- Almighty Creator God, I pray in the precious and holy name of Jesus Christ, my Savior, that You put an impenetrable hedge of spiritual protection around [name] through this Satanic holiday so that all efforts by the cult to contact her will be blocked.

Sometimes Christian therapists allow, or even encourage, support people to accompany survivors during therapy sessions. This not only enables supporters to follow-up with the survivors much more knowledgeably after the session, but it also gives them the opportunity to provide emotional and spiritual support *during* the session. In this way they can engage in the exact type of spiritual warfare needed as the session progresses. This is extremely valuable as Satan's greatest efforts to hinder the release of survivors are often unleashed in their therapy sessions.

Specific spiritual warfare needs arising during therapy may include:

- Binding the ability of demons to block truth and healing,
- Binding the ability of demons to hear pertinent information and respond to any therapeutic advance in any adverse way,
- Binding demons which prohibit alters from speaking,
- Binding demonic guards blocking access to significant memories or alters,
- Binding demons that may hinder alters from hearing God's voice of truth,
- Unmasking deceptive demonic imagery,
- Binding demons from interfering as alters remember and renounce the legal grounds which provide the demonic attachment(s),
- Expelling demons once their legal grounds are renounced.

Your willingness to support a survivor in spiritual warfare will reap significant benefits for yourself as well as the survivor. You will undoubtedly grow in your understanding of the spiritual realm and will have the opportunity to apply your knowledge of spiritual warfare in a perhaps unprecedented way. You will also share the joyous rewards of seeing the power of God free the survivor from Satan's grip and then of observing the changes that occur in her life as a result.

Bible Study and Discipleship

Spiritual support can also potentially involve instructing and strengthening survivors and their alters in the truths of God's Word. This is especially crucial for alters who have been demonized and/or extensively indoctrinated by the cult. If spiritual growth does not occur for alters after deliverance, demons may return and actually bring the survivor into greater bondage than before (Luke 11:24-26).

The cult works hard to impugn the character and trustworthiness of God in the minds of the alters with whom they work. Replacing these misrepresentations with truth from God's Word is essential both before and after cult-loyal alters put their faith in God. Sometimes false beliefs can be challenged by bringing them directly to God for assessment. Often He will impress the truth on the mind of the alter in such a poignant way that it instantly eliminates all doubt.

When parts of the survivor's system are already grounded in spiritual truth, they can often spread truth internally to those alters who have renounced their allegiance to Satan and desire to follow God instead. Truth also spreads very naturally when alters are fused or integrated with more spiritually mature parts of the system.

Whether from God, other alters, or willing supporters; cult-indoctrinated alters need to understand and experience the *true* nature of God and learn the privileges of being His child. They need to discover and claim His many promises to them. They also need to learn the importance of faith and prayer as well as the elements of effective spiritual warfare so they can successfully defend themselves against Satan's efforts to bring them back under his bondage. In addition, they need to learn the importance of ridding their lives of sin and filling them with the Holy Spirit.

When considerable demonization is present, discussion of spiritual issues can sometimes create significant disturbance in the system. Some survivors cannot even attend church because of the degree of internal torment and punishment they receive. Under these conditions spiritual instruction must be handled with great care, usually by a Christian therapist or a well-trained pastor or layperson who will focus only on those issues which may be impeding the progress of therapy. As counseling and deliverance progresses, internal opposition to spiritual truth will generally lessen, and the system will become more cooperative in allowing spiritual instruction from other sources as well.

Regardless of what overt spiritual instruction the system will tolerate, discipleship often takes place best in the context of everyday life experiences. Short, succinct statements relevant to a current situation can catch the system off guard and have a profound effect on the alters who are present or listening. You may discover other creative means to expose parts of an otherwise resistant system to God's truth, such as strategically placed notes, cards, or plaques. While you must always be sensitive to any evidence of opposition when doing these things, the survivor's system is usually much less apt to react to these brief, unexpected and indirect bursts of spiritual education than to deliberately set up times for overt Bible study.

Chapter Nine

Material Support

Another type of support survivors often need is what I am calling "material support." This entails contributing your own resources to help the survivor in various non-therapeutic needs she may have, including finances, transportation, child care, housing, and/or assistance with certain aspects of daily living.

Remember that every good deed you do or every sacrifice you make stores up treasure for yourself in heaven (1 Tim. 6:18-19). Your generosity to others—whether of your time, your possessions, or your finances—opens the door for you to receive the same generosity in your time of need (Luke 6:38; Heb. 6:10). You never lose your reward for giving even a cup of cold water to one of God's needy children (Matt. 10:42).

Financial Support

Because treatment for DID is a lengthy—and usually expensive—process, the financial resources of many survivors get depleted long before their healing is complete. Those who are unemployed and/or living on their own generally experience this need most critically, but others too may eventually need some form of financial assistance.

While you may not be able to meet this need entirely on your own, you can perhaps approach your church or share the need with an appropriate group that might be willing to contribute collectively to this need. You can also help the survivor connect to whatever social service resources may be available to help her make ends meet.

Assistance with Daily Living

Functionality among multiples varies greatly. Some are super-achievers maintaining high level jobs while others are significantly disabled. Most will find, however, that their ability to function well decreases somewhat as therapy intensifies. The saying that it sometimes "gets worse before it gets better" generally applies when dealing with multiples having a history of severe childhood abuse. Therapy can often be paced, however, to minimize such a decrease in functionality. Therefore, if you, as a supporter, see this occurring, you may want to report it to the therapist, who can possibly slow the pace of therapy down a little to prevent incapacitating the survivor.

Being too overwhelmed emotionally to function adequately is not uncommon for survivors from time to time. If they have small children at home, this can pose a significant problem. Therefore, they may welcome somebody taking care of the children for awhile so they can rest or try to "pull things together." Even if they are able to function adequately, mothers with dependent children will often welcome the opportunity to have some time alone to process new information or work with their alter systems. This can be especially helpful immediately following therapy sessions.

Some less functional survivors may need help on a regular basis with certain essential tasks of life, especially when a supportive spouse is not in the picture. If the survivor's system is particularly unstable for any reason, she may need assistance with such things as shopping, paying bills, or keeping various appointments. Frequent switching can sometimes disrupt the consistency needed to carry out these tasks.

Visits to the doctor can be particularly stressful for survivors, often precipitating instability and switching. This is not only confusing to the doctor and embarrassing to the survivor, but it can also hinder important communication between them. Child alters can be especially frightened of doctors' visits and may need comfort and reassurance that no abuse will occur. Having a knowledgeable friend accompany the survivor on these occasions to provide this input and support, as well as assure adequate communication, is often helpful.

If parts of the survivor's system interfere with her ability to get to therapy appointments on time, having someone to drive her there may also be beneficial. At other times her emotional state may render her unable or unsafe to drive, and she will appreciate having volunteers temporarily provide transportation for her.

Occasionally survivors may need temporary housing as well if their finances are extremely tight or they are unsafe to be left on their own. Opening your home to a survivor must be done with considerable foresight, however, as it will significantly alter the dynamics of life for all those in the home. Therefore, you must carefully consider the needs and safety of other family members as well as your own priorities in making this decision, particularly if minor children are still in the home.

If you do invite a survivor to live with you, try to think through as many potential problems that might occur as possible. If you know someone else that has taken in a survivor, talk to them about the problems they have had to address. Remember that pulling back in any way from the survivor after the arrangement begins is apt to be viewed as rejection or as a "you're bad" pronouncement. Therefore, make sure the survivor understands what you are and are not offering or promising her, and set specific boundaries and "rules" very clearly from the beginning. This might include what areas of the house are in or out of bounds, what kitchen privileges are allowed, what responsibilities she is expected to carry out, what activities are required or forbidden, and how much time you will be able to spend with her personally.

Also, determine what types of situations will instantly terminate the arrangement. This could include any violence or threats made against household members or any cultic rituals taking place in the home. You might even decide that self-harm or suicide attempts are unacceptable and will require immediate hospitalization.

Of utmost importance is that you not provide an environment that is so indulgent that the survivor would much rather maintain the status quo than work toward returning to a healthy independence. Therefore, from the very beginning establish healthy goals which, when reached, will "graduate" the survivor back to independent living, and try to set a reasonable time frame in which to accomplish this. Also, set up regular intervals, either monthly or quarterly, for re-evaluating the arrangement. Never leave a live-in situation open-ended. The survivor must recognize this as a sacrificial move on your part and is not intended to go on forever.

Whether the survivor lives with you not, whenever giving material support of any kind, be careful not to overreact or "baby" the survivor. Allow her to be as responsible as possible for her own needs. Overdoing in this area of support can contribute to keeping her in a dependent state, which is counterproductive to her healing.

Chapter Ten

Therapeutic Support

Professional counseling can cost up to $80 or $90 an hour or more. Even at reduced rates, the fee can be prohibitive to survivors without insurance or other significant financial resources. Furthermore, the number of professional counselors and psychologists knowledgeable of the unique dynamics involved in DID and ritual abuse is currently insufficient to accommodate the ever-increasing number of multiples seeking help. Those able to recognize and address the spiritual components involved are even fewer.

In light of these problems, alternative sources of therapy are necessary. While it is admittedly not a totally ideal option, certain willing laypersons can be trained to do effective work with multiples. Many who can secure help in no other way are eternally grateful for pastors and other willing laymen who have stepped in to help bridge the gap.

The truth is that most of the professionals working with this clientele obtained their knowledge of the unique dynamics of DID and ritual abuse directly from the survivors themselves. While laymen may lack the broader psychological expertise of trained clinicians, they can also learn much directly from survivors. They can also draw upon other available resources, such as literature, seminars, and consultations with more experienced therapists or lay ministers. Because of the complexities involved in this diagnosis, a vast amount of networking occurs in this field with counselors sharing their own knowledge and experience with each other. Anyone eager to learn can get connected to this network quite easily.

Providing therapy for multiples is definitely not for everyone. Those considering this possibility must themselves be in reasonably good health—psychologically, emotionally, and spiritually—or their own unresolved issues will interfere with their ability to do good therapy. Being disciplined in setting and maintaining good personal boundaries is also extremely important. The very nature of DID requires that those who work with such clients be comfortable with handling all emotions and personality types as well as a wide range of sexual discussions. Skillfulness in interpersonal relationships is a must as well as commitment, sensitivity, love, and compassion.

This type of therapy is never easy. Those embarking upon it must be prepared for a long and challenging journey which will stretch them in many ways. It will require a substantial investment of time, both in becoming educated and in working with the survivor(s). The opportunity to learn in an apprentice-type relationship with a more experienced clinician is the ideal way to be trained in this specialized form of therapy but is not always possible.

Through whatever means, the potential counselor must become familiar with the basic dynamics of DID and ritual abuse; the long-term effects of trauma and sexual abuse; the role of conflict, denial, and false beliefs in producing DID; and the dynamics of the system structure, programming, and demonization. He or she will also need to develop skills in crisis management, conflict resolution, spiritual warfare, and deliverance. Other necessary skills include establishing rapport and trust with a broad range of personality types; identifying and bringing truth to false beliefs; processing memories to heal pain, inactivate programming, and eliminate the need for dissociation; and teaching healthy living and coping skills.

If God lays it upon your heart to assume a therapeutic role with a survivor, He will guide you and sustain you through the process. Never assume such a role lightly, however, or without a definite calling from God.

Chapter Eleven

Support Versus Caretaking

While abuse survivors may appear to be extremely needy people, those desiring to help them recover from the painful tragedies in their lives must avoid falling into the trap of codependency. Feeling so sorry for them that you rush in to do everything possible to help them and to demonstrate your love for them is not necessarily the best approach. Taking on care which the survivor can provide for herself will almost always be counterproductive.

Survivors certainly need good Christian love, but it must be given in a way that is truly beneficial and doesn't perpetuate their staying in a victim role. While this was obviously their position as children, a major goal of the treatment process is to bring them out of their victim mentality. This is why the term "survivor" is used so extensively with those who have suffered abuse.

Therefore, be very cautious of extending such an intense level of care or nurture that the survivor would rather bask in the "luxury" of it than work on her recovery. You don't want her to feel that she has too much to lose in the way of care if she "gets well." If at any time you sense that you and/or her therapist are more invested in her healing than she herself is, this situation needs to be addressed.

The primary responsibility for recovery must always be on the survivor. Some survivors seem to think that their getting well depends on everyone else doing the right things for them. This is a totally false perspective and will be fatal to their healing process. Getting well involves hard mental and emotional work by the survivor herself. A therapist can guide her and you can support her, but no one can get in her head and fix it for her. She must do that herself, and because it is hard work, she must be strongly motivated if she is to be successful.

As you extend support to the survivor, make sure that you are taking care of yourself to the same extent that you are caring for her. Because most abuse survivors lack an understanding of correct boundary setting and self-care, your modeling these crucial dynamics will benefit them immensely in the long run.

Also, as tempting as it may be, do not try to become substitute "parents" for child alters. Help them grieve what they did not receive as children in the way of adequate parenting and learn to care for themselves as adults. Even more importantly, try to identify what beliefs or issues keep them separated from the Core Self.

I in no way want to minimize the need for genuine compassion and validation of the immense pain and difficult struggles which survivors experience. Just don't be a rescuer—because that keeps them in the victim role. Although having someone else take care of them may *feel* so good and you may think that *deserve* it so much, it will not help them move towards greater health. Therefore, keep your focus on supporting in a way that empowers them rather than makes them more dependent on others for their needs.

Chapter Twelve

The Role of the Church

The role of the Church in supporting abuse survivors, especially ritual abuse survivors, is a sensitive and often controversial issue, yet one that needs to be addressed. If the Church truly functioned as the Body of Christ, survivors would seemingly find within its doors the same acceptance, compassion, nurture, and assistance that Jesus Christ Himself would give them.

Certainly the Church *seems like* the most logical place for these wounded individuals to find refuge, support, and spiritual instruction as they seek inner healing and battle to free themselves from Satan's hold on their lives. In actual experience, however, ritual abuse survivors often discover that the Church has little understanding of the realities of DID, ritual abuse, or demonization and is totally unprepared for dealing with them.

The end result is that many ritual abuse survivors feel not only misunderstood but sometimes rejected or even mistreated by the Church. If this occurs repeatedly in church after church, they may eventually become totally disillusioned with the Church as an effective resource for their healing.

This is tragic for both the churches and the survivors and must certainly grieve the heart of God as well. When a church fails to function as a true representation of Christ and His character to all who enter its doors, it fails its responsibility to God and will one day be held accountable for this neglect (Mat. 25:44-45; 1 Cor. 3:12-15). In addition, it misses the blessings and opportunities for growth that God perhaps intended its members to receive through ministering to these wounded, but special, children of His.

It is tragic for survivors because all too often they interpret the failure of the Church as a failure of God's love for them. Feeling abandoned by both the Church and God, they may easily eliminate the most powerful resource they have for their healing.

The dramatic conversion of their cult-loyal alters may also be jeopardized. Often they were persuaded to make the mammoth decision of changing their allegiance from Satan to God because they were told that not only does God offer them forgiveness and freedom, but also that those in His kingdom operate with love and compassion. If they do not find that promised love and compassion in the Church, they may feel deceived or tricked, making the Kingdom of God no more appealing to them than Satan's realm.

While most survivors can accept that not everyone in a given church has the time, emotional capacity, and spiritual maturity to understand and reach out to them, they have difficulty grasping that *no one* can. Why should those with more "normal" needs be received more readily than they? Why should they feel rejected because they are too unusual or extreme in their needs? Jesus would not have turned His back on them. Why should His people?

These poignant questions, while valid, are not necessarily easy to answer. The reasons for the Church's failure to minister adequately to survivors of severe abuse are quite varied. Some are legitimate and understandable, stemming from a lack of knowledge or experience in dealing with their often complex issues or needs or from spiritual immaturity. In the case of ritual abuse survivors, believers who are not well grounded in the Word are sometimes terrified of dealing with anything that has to do with Satan or demons. Others are unwilling to extend themselves beyond their own self-inscribed comfort zones or to be obedient to the Lord.

Other problems are more philosophical in nature. The church's leadership may not believe in "recovered memories" or the depth of human depravity and sexual perversion they reveal.

They may not believe in Satan's active pursuit of world domination or in covert government mind-control experiments. Some may not believe that Christians can be demonized, or they believe that alter-identities are really demons.

The truth is that ritual abuse survivors and churches both face a major dilemma when they confront each other. If the survivor has already had a bad experience in another church, she may struggle with whether to reveal her diagnosis as a multiple or her history of ritual abuse to *this* church. If she does, she risks the possibility of further misunderstanding, conflict, and rejection with its accompanying pain.

On the other hand, if she chooses to hide her diagnosis and history from the church, she will have to remain very superficial in her relationships and will constantly feel that she is hiding a big secret about who she really is. People in the church may be perplexed by the inconsistencies in her behavior, her memory, or even her spiritual beliefs as different alters switch in and out. They may also be baffled by her sometimes peculiar reactions and not know how to respond.

In addition, she greatly decreases the possibility of getting any of her legitimate spiritual needs related to her ritual abuse met in the church. She will never know if perhaps some individuals in *this* church might truly be willing to embrace her for who she really is and genuinely try to help her.

The church's dilemma, if a ritual abuse survivor does make herself known, is even more complex. If they don't support her, they offend the survivor, contribute to her negative image of the Church, and renege on their responsibility as the Body of Christ. If they do openly support her, they risk potential division in the church, which could arise because of the controversial nature of the issues involved; because of a fear of anything demonic; or because of the inordinate amount time, personnel, or other resources directed to just one or several individuals.

Having a known ritual abuse survivor in the church generally forces the church leadership into a multi-leveled series of decisions.

Because they are most likely not well-informed on this subject, they must first decide if they are willing to make an effort to understand DID and ritual abuse. If they are, they must find a reputable source to bring them this knowledge. After becoming informed, they must then determine whether they are willing to accept the realities of dissociation, recovered memories, and demonization.

If they *are* willing to embrace these realities, they proceed to the next level of decisions, which concern the nature and extent of their involvement in supporting such survivors. Virtually any church should be willing to provide acceptance, love, and prayer support. If increasing numbers of churches across the country were willing to do this alone, it would be a great start and tremendously encouraging to survivors.

Some churches may be willing to go further in helping survivors on their healing journeys, however. In order to make this decision, they must carefully evaluate the extent of their available resources of time, personnel, and finances to devote in this direction. They also need to consider where in priority such a ministry would fit in the overall objectives of their church.

If they agree to move forward into more of a ministry role with survivors, they must then decide who will be involved and how they will be equipped. They also need to decide the parameters of support they are willing to offer. Will they help with daily living needs if they arise? What about financial needs? Are they willing to create a special prayer chain for survivors' needs? Will they be available in times of crisis?

If the church does not have an adequate counselor on staff, will they help survivors get good Christian therapy elsewhere? Is the pastor or another leader willing to interact with the survivors' therapists to enhance understanding and coordinate support or other interventions on their behalf? Is the church willing to participate in deliverance, spiritual instruction, and/or discipleship for these individuals?

The final level of decision that church leaders must make involves how open to be with the entire church body about its ministry to ritual abuse survivors. Just because *they* have wrestled through the controversial issues involved doesn't mean that everyone in their congregation has. Therefore, they need a measure of foresight regarding the particular problems that could arise in the body as a consequence of this ministry.

Unfortunately, some groups have created considerable media hype challenging the accuracy of "recovered memories." Without being knowledgeable of the mechanism of dissociation and how the mind handles *traumatic* memories differently than ordinary memories, the general population has no sound basis on which to evaluate this issue.

Another closely related concern is the reliability of the allegations that ritual abuse survivors make regarding the identity of cult perpetrators. These might potentially even be made towards other church members, which would understandably precipitate a significant crisis for the church leaders.

The subject of demonization, with the fears and questions it raises, is another potentially divisive issue in some churches. Many Christians seemingly desire to remain ignorant of this reality and may be hostile to anyone whom they perceive is "finding demons behind every bush." Many believers are also absolutely convinced that Christians cannot possibly "have demons." Others may err on the other side and insist that a survivor's entire problem is demonic, believing that her alter-identities are really demons.

At some point the amount of resources going towards such a small segment of the congregation may also seem inordinate. This could potentially cause problems too, especially if the church is small.

In light of all of these complicating factors, the most workable solution for supporting ritual abuse survivors within a church seems to be through a team which maintains a low-profile in the church body. In this way neither the specialized ministry itself nor the issues it raises need interface with the entire congregation. It also allows survivors to have a small group of people with whom they can be "real" while at the same time being more protective of what they reveal to the majority of the church.

Because supporting abuse survivors can sometimes be demanding, time consuming, and draining, having a team enables the load to be spread among a number of individuals so that no one of them gets burned out. A team also enables supporters to serve in the area of their particular gifts rather than trying to be a "jack of all trades" to the survivor. If some are unable to become deeply involved emotionally, they can still be of assistance in providing things such as prayer support, discipleship, or transportation when needed.

Selecting potential members for such a team often occurs quite naturally if some in the church have already begun reaching out to the survivor. The pastor or church leaders can also judiciously approach other individuals they feel may be suitable.

After being presented with the need and receiving a limited introduction and exposure to DID/ritual abuse issues, this initial pool of hand-picked individuals can then decide whether God would have them commit to actual participation on the team. Service must always be voluntary and on an "as able" basis.

Those who choose to be a part of this special ministry can then receive whatever further training is appropriate for the level of involvement they are willing to have. This could come through reading, attending seminars, and/or interacting with other more knowledgeable people, including the survivor(s).

At some point the various team members should meet together and define their particular roles with the survivor(s). This will help to organize the necessary tasks involved and enable each member to operate most effectively within their particular giftedness and comfort zones.

Becoming involved in supporting abuse survivors will of necessity be a "learn as you go" situation for most churches, but what a help and encouragement they will be to the survivors they support! What joy they will also bring to the Father's heart! They will not lose their reward!

Chapter Thirteen

Spiritual Protection

Whenever Christians become actively involved in advancing the Kingdom of God or freeing captives from the dominion of Satan, they can expect heightened efforts by Satan and his forces to hinder their success. Therefore, if you commit yourself to helping a ritual abuse survivor obtain freedom from her spiritual bondages, you must be prepared for this possibility. It need not evoke fear, however, as long as you understand the nature of the enemy, the battle he is waging, and the spiritual armor that can effectively foil his attacks.

As the reigning "prince" of the kingdom of darkness, Satan is a real being with supernatural power and intelligence, originally one of the highest created entities among the angelic hosts (Ezek. 28:12-15; Eph. 2:2). Having lost his personal challenge of God's supremacy in the heavenlies (Isa. 14:12-15), his sights now seem to be set on gaining supremacy on earth.

While Satan may believe that he initiated his plan himself, God is the Mastermind behind his very existence. The absolute supremacy of God demands that He created, situated, and equipped Satan to serve *His own purpose* (Col. 1:16).

In order to understand this purpose, one must grasp the "big picture" of God's love and His plan for mankind. Love is the very essence of God's being (1 John 4:8, 16). Love, by its very nature, is meaningless apart from relationship, however.

This is where the creation of man comes in. God created man to receive and to reciprocate His love! In other words, *He created us to be the fulfillment of His divine love nature!* What greater destiny could we possibly have? No wonder God calls us His glorious inheritance (Eph. 1:18)! No wonder He created us in such a distinctive manner—in His own image and with His own breath (Gen. 1:27; 2:7)!

God's love, rooted in the very core of His being, is given universally and unconditionally. All man needs to do is to receive it (John 1:12; 3:16). The deep yearning of God's heart, however, is that man not only *receive* His love but that he also *reciprocate* it in fullest measure (Mat. 22:37). God's effort to woo man into such a relationship with Himself forms the heart of the entire Scriptures, and it is within this context that His purpose for Satan is embedded.

Because love is most genuine when it is voluntarily given, God created man with a free will. Then, because love also has greatest significance when the object of devotion is chosen from a "playing field" of other potentially appealing options, God provided Satan, originally known as Lucifer, as an alternative object of devotion for man.

Obviously, any alternative to God Himself would also have to be a powerfully alluring, supernatural being. Therefore, God created Lucifer as "the model of perfection, full of wisdom and perfect in beauty," abiding on the very "mount of God" (Ezek. 28:12-15).

In this highly elevated position, however, Lucifer felt so powerful, so privileged, and so close to God that he arrogantly aspired *to be like God* (Isa. 14:13-14). Therefore, he rebelled against serving God and set his course on challenging God's supremacy.

God's sovereignty is as sure as His love, however. Therefore, Satan suffered immediate defeat in the heavenly realm, resulting in his demotion from the "mount of God" (Ezek. 28:16-17) and his name being changed from Lucifer, Son of the Morning, to Satan, the Adversary.

This may have temporarily dampened Satan's ambitions, but it effectively moved him towards God's intended role for him. As soon as the earth was created, with man as its crowning jewel, Satan had a new domain in which to seek supremacy. First, however, he would have to gain man's allegiance—which put Satan precisely into the competitive role for the devotion of mankind that God had ordained for him.

In order for Satan to serve as a viable substitute for man's devotion, God did not thoroughly strip him of power, authority, or resources when He demoted him within the heavenly realms. Instead, He allowed Satan to retain a vast following of (evil) spiritual beings that serve under his command (Eph. 6:12). He also gave him a limited, temporary authority over the spiritual realm known in Scripture as the "kingdom of the air" (Eph. 2:1-2). To further "level the playing field," God created man with the ability to sin, along with the ability to love, thus giving him the potential to fulfill either God's or Satan's agenda.

Before God allowed an initial showdown with His rival to take place, however, He gave Adam and Eve a significant taste of His love. He began by preparing an ideal habitat for them to live in, the beautiful Garden of Eden. While requiring them to cultivate and care for the garden, God lavishly provided their needs and enjoyed an intimate relationship with them there, seemingly meeting and conversing with them on a regular basis. He also treated them with dignity and respect. He honored them by giving them authority over His entire earthly creation, including the privilege of naming all the animals and birds in it (Gen. 1:26, 28; 2:8-9, 19-20; 3:8). All of this must certainly have endeared them to Him!

To test the genuineness of their devotion to Him, however, God gave them one restriction (John 14:15, 21). He told them not to eat from the Tree of the Knowledge of Good and Evil—lest they die (Gen. 2:16-17). Providing this opportunity for disobedience and then allowing Satan to have access to them in the garden were both essential to His plan.

Recognizing all that was at stake, Satan lost no time in presenting himself in stunning fashion and challenging God's commitment to Adam and Eve's well-being, specifically in the restriction He gave them concerning eating from the forbidden tree. Satan then put his own spin on the meaning of the tree's name and the consequences of eating its fruit. Unfortunately, both Adam and Eve chose to believe Satan rather than to obey God.

The impact of Satan's victory in this crucial first round of His competitive quest for man's allegiance was immense. Adam and Eve's ill-fated choice activated their inherent sin nature, caused them to lose their intimate relationship with God, and brought not only themselves but the entire human race from that time forward under the penalty of death and the dominion of Satan (Rom. 5:12; 6:16; Acts 26:18). By gaining dominion over man, Satan also gained control of what would become the world system of government, a major trophy in his pursuit of world domination (Luke 4:5-6; John 12:31; 1 John 5:19).

Through Satan's newly acquired position of authority over man, he also gained access to man's deep, inner drives (known in the New Testament Scriptures as the "flesh") and was able to warp them for his own advantage (Rom. 8:7-8; Gal. 5:17-21; 2 Tim. 2:26). This is when man's heart became "desperately wicked" (Jer. 17:9; KJV). This was not how God created it, but how Satan corrupted it (cf. Gen. 1:31).

With every succeeding generation of mankind being born by default into the kingdom of darkness with an active sin nature, the deck seemed to become quickly stacked in Satan's favor. God never lost His sovereignty over the entire situation, however. The book of Job wondrously pulls back the curtain of heaven and allows us to see that Satan is only allowed to affect man's life within definite parameters set by God (Job 1:9—2:6). He is never given totally free reign. This inspired account also reveals how greatly God delights in those whose devotion to Himself remains steadfast in spite of the temporary concessions He has given to Satan (Job 1:1; 2:3, 10; 13:15).

God knew that allowing Satan to become his competitor would potentially bring great suffering to both Himself and His beloved human race. He also knew, however, that in the crucible of suffering, love achieves a sterling quality. Therefore, "for the joy set before Him" (Heb. 12:2; NASB), He did not retreat from His predetermined course to gain His prized inheritance (Eph. 1: 18)—a reciprocal love relationship with man.

Once man came under the dominion of Satan, God could redeem him in only one way—by sending His own Son to pay the penalty of death on man's behalf (1 Cor. 15:22; Eph. 1:7; Col. 1:13-14; Titus 2:13-14). When He willingly made this supreme sacrifice of love, He effectively restored to man the same freedom of choice that Adam and Eve had in the Garden of Eden regarding the object of their devotion and their eternal destiny. By doing nothing, man remains under the dominion of Satan. All it takes, however, to enter an everlasting love relationship with God is a simple act of repentance and faith, personally accepting Christ's sacrificial death for *one's own sins* (Luke 24:46-47; John 1:12; 3:16; Eph. 2:8).

When man makes this momentous decision and is redeemed by the shed blood of Jesus, God immediately turns the tables on Satan and equips the Christian for victory over him in all his avenues of operation. Through the awesome gift of the Holy Spirit to every believer (Rom. 8:9; 1 Cor. 6:19), God shares with us His own divine nature, giving us the capacity to overcome both the sinful drives of the flesh and the illusive attraction of our corrupt world, which is under Satan's control (Gal. 5:16; 2 Pet. 1:4; 1 John 5:19).

God even allows us to share the position of spiritual authority that He has granted to the risen Lord Jesus Christ over all the powers of darkness (Eph. 1:19-23; 2:6). This means that whenever we recognize an evil spiritual attack, we can use the authority of the name of Jesus Christ to command the obedience of whatever evil forces are involved (Luke 10:17; Acts 16:18).

Unfortunately, our enemy knows he has no chance against such a powerful *offensive* blow. Therefore, he works very craftily to weaken our spiritual defenses and then expertly camouflages his arrows, hoping they will sneak in unnoticed. For this reason God also provides us with clear instructions on how to put on a spiritual "suit of armor" which will effectively protect us from Satan's attacks, however subtle or disguised they may be (Eph. 6:10-17).

If we are to keep Satan's arrows from piercing our souls and debilitating our spiritual strength and effectiveness in ministry, we must understand the nature of each piece of this armor and how to keep it effectively in place. This armor is not an automatic inheritance received at the time of salvation or God would not instruct us to "put it on." It is also not something we can don "once and for all" subsequent to salvation; nor can we quickly equip ourselves with it by merely repeating the words of Ephesians 6:14-17 as we begin the day. Rather, the spiritual armor represents specific character qualities which we must develop and consistently manifest in our daily lives. This is what determines the effectiveness of our defense against Satan.

The Belt of Truth

Scripture describes Satan as a **liar** (John 8:44) and a **deceiver** (Rev. 12:9 KJV), yet one who disguises himself as an "angel of light" (2 Cor. 11:14). He is extremely adept at transforming lies to appear as truth, garbing them with tantalizing allurement, and expertly camouflaging their diabolical source as he did so well in the Garden of Eden (Gen. 3:1-5). He loves to implant niggling doubts, subtle half-truths, false condemnations, unfounded fears, and deceptive thoughts in our minds to diminish our spiritual strength. His tactics are so smooth that without keen sensitivity in our spirits we might easily attribute the origin of these inner messages to ourselves (Mat. 16:21-23; 2 Cor. 10:5; James 3:14-16).

If you enter a supportive relationship with a wounded individual, you must be alert for possible arrows of deception that Satan may direct at each of you. This is particularly true when involved with ritual abuse survivors as Satan is deeply invested in defeating their attempts to gain freedom from his bondage.

In your own mind He may try to excite fears and false suspicions of either the survivor or the cult, or he may instigate doubts of your adequacy to be of service to her. If he cannot pull you completely away from her, he may use other implanted lies to diminish your effectiveness in helping her.

In the survivor's mind Satan has undoubtedly already instilled many erroneous thoughts, beliefs, and fears designed to keep her in bondage. Some of these may have been deliberately implanted or augmented by perpetrators who wanted her to believe she had no recourse but to submit to their control. Frequently, cult perpetrators also make a special effort to persuade survivors that they are cut off from God and cannot avail themselves of His divine resources.

Satan may also work to amplify a survivor's sense of guilt, shame, or defilement in an effort to undermine her self-worth as well as her perception of acceptance by God or worthiness of His forgiveness. These lies could potentially drive her to hopelessness, despair, or even suicide. At the very least they will rob her of the supernatural peace, joy, and confidence which are hers through the Holy Spirit as a child of God (Gal. 5:22-23).

Because Satan's tactics are based so strongly on deception, the first piece of armor that God tells us to gird ourselves with is the Belt of Truth (Eph. 6:14). Truth is one of the strongest weapons against Satan in the spiritual realm. He cannot stand against truth, especially the truths of God's Word. Through quoted Scripture alone Jesus totally defeated Satan when tempted by him in the wilderness (Mat. 4:1-11).

We can do the same but only as we build a personal arsenal of truth in our own hearts and minds. For this reason God instructs us to meditate on His Word daily so its truths can be implanted and stored in our hearts (Josh. 1:8; Ps. 1:1-3; 119:11; John 17:17). The more we know of God's truth, the better equipped we will be in recognizing and refuting Satan's deceptions.

In order to gain the full protection of the Belt of Truth, however, we must not only *know* truth; we must also *practice* it (James 1:22-25). We must allow it to transform our minds (Rom. 12:2) and direct our lives (Ps. 119:105) so that it becomes a distinguishing mark of our character.

Perhaps the most critical, and yet most vulnerable, aspect of our lives to be governed by truth is our speech. James aptly describes the key role that speech plays in reflecting moral character and determining the course of one's life. Using multiple analogies, he also warns about the tremendous potential for evil it embodies. If we do not carefully guard our speech and keep it consistently in line with truth, it can be used by Satan to create inestimable damage in our own lives as well as in our entire sphere of influence (James 3:2-12).

In His Sermon on the Mount, Jesus revealed God's standard for our speech in no uncertain terms: "Simply let your 'Yes' be 'Yes,' and 'No,' 'No'; anything beyond this *comes from the evil one"* (Matthew 5:37 NIV). How much clearer could He inform us that even the slightest deviation from truth in our speech comes from Satan, who is truly the "father of lies" (John 8:44)? When we yield to Satan's temptation to bend or alter the truth, we essentially trade our Belt of Truth for one of Satan's key artillery pieces—deception (James 3:6; Rev. 12:9)!

Satan, of course, is delighted to lend us one of his weapons, especially in exchange for part of our defensive armor. However, he rarely lends out a piece of his artillery without one of his "soldiers" (demons) hovering nearby to coach us in its use. The more accustomed we become to using dishonesty, the more comfortable it feels and the deeper Satan digs his foothold in our soul.

With diabolical astuteness Satan gives us seemingly legitimate reasons to justify twisting the truth "just a little." Some may even seem godly in nature. Maybe we don't want to offend someone or "rock the boat." Perhaps we believe it will shelter or protect someone from pain or embarrassment—maybe even ourselves. We may start altering or exaggerating the truth to make a greater impact on people, seeing no harm in misrepresenting a situation as long as it doesn't hurt anyone.

These are all lies of the enemy! We must trust God that absolute truth is *always* the right course to take in *every* situation. When we are obedient to Him in speaking truth, we can trust Him with the consequences.

Truth is most powerful when spoken in love (Eph. 4:15). If we use truth to shame, humiliate, or embarrass someone or deliver it with vengeful anger, we mix the godly power of truth with fleshly characteristics tainted by the enemy. This sends greatly conflicting messages and rarely produces positive results.

The Breastplate of Righteousness

Although sin no longer determines our eternal destiny once we have been redeemed by the blood of Jesus, it does have a major impact on our spiritual health and the integrity of our spiritual armor. Therefore, one of Satan's greatest strategies is to entice us to sin. He knows that sin will hinder our intimacy with God and our access to His power through prayer (Ps. 24:3-5; 34:15-16; 66:18; 1 John 1:6-7).

Willfully engaging in sin (James 4:17) is so crippling to our defensive strength in the spiritual realm that it is seemingly analogous to exposing our heart to the enemy. For this reason God instructs us to keep our life-sustaining chest area covered with the Breastplate of Righteousness (Eph. 6:14). Since this is a righteousness that we are to "put on" (Eph. 6:13), I believe that it refers to the consistent practice of righteousness in our daily lives rather than to the righteousness of Christ with which we are permanently covered when we place our faith in Him for salvation (Rom. 3:21-22; Phil. 3:8-9).

While sin is often blatantly obvious, at other times it can be very subtle and even camouflaged as a seeming righteousness. Satan is quite masterful in counterfeiting the righteousness of God in a person's life. The Pharisees in the Gospels provide a prime example of this (Mat. 23:1-28). By dutifully aligning their behavior to a legalistic code of conduct, they produced the *appearance* of a godly lifestyle. Jesus, however, referred to them as "sons of hell" (Mat. 23:15; NASB), clearly indicating the source of their "pseudo-righteousness."

Christians today can fall into this same legalistic trap if they concentrate on merely following godly "rules" of conduct rather than allowing true righteousness to flow spontaneously from a heart submitted to the Holy Spirit. While subtle, this important difference can significantly affect one's defensive strength against the enemy (Gal. 3:1-5).

Keeping our Breastplates of Righteousness in place takes a committed effort on our part. God, however, has provided powerful resources to help us do this. One of the greatest is the gift of His own Holy Spirit to live within every believer (1 Cor. 6:19; 2 Cor. 1:21-22; 5:5).

His constant presence in us gives us the potential to triumph over the flesh and its sinful desires. We are no longer in total bondage to this Satan-corrupted part of our being (Eph. 2:1-3). Our hearts now hear the inner beat of two drummers, one coming from the flesh, which continues to pant after the deceptive allurements of self-gratification, and the other from the Holy Spirit, who yearns to synchronize our spirits with His own divine nature. Our job is to learn to distinguish the two, resist the lustful passions of the flesh, and allow the Holy Spirit to be the true "drum major" of our lives. This is the way God has provided to enable us to escape the corruption of our flesh as well as the temptations of the evil one and the world system he operates (Rom. 8:5-9; Gal. 5:16; 2 Pet. 1:4; 1 John 5:19).

In addition to the Holy Spirit, another vitally important resource God has given us to help keep our Breastplates of Righteousness consistently in place is the Word of God. As we study and meditate on it, God's standard of righteousness can penetrate deep within our hearts and minds, purifying our lives and enhancing our ability to recognize sin (Josh. 1:8, Ps. 1:2-3; 119:9, 11; John 15:3).

Of course, no one can live a totally sinless life. Because of the ongoing presence of the flesh, even the most dedicated of

Christians will inevitable fall prey to sin (Rom. 7:14-25). Here again the Holy Spirit serves an important role in sounding an internal alarm to alert us to the error of our ways. Our part is to be sensitive to His uncomfortable tug within our spirits and confess our sins to God. When we do, our fellowship with Him and our privileges before His throne are instantly restored, and our Breastplates of Righteousness are returned to their protective positions against the assaults of the enemy (John 16:8; 1 John 1:6–2:2).

The Boots of Peace

Sturdy, protective footwear enables a soldier to brace himself against an enemy attack or maneuver quickly over rough terrain without damage to his feet. In spiritual warfare our battlefield boots are found in the full appropriation of the Gospel of Peace (Eph. 6:15).

On a very foundational level our faith in the Gospel message of Jesus Christ's sacrificial death on the Cross for our sins secures our peace with God (Rom. 5:1). Our sins are forgiven and no longer separate us from Him. We are released from God's wrath, freed from Satan's dominion, and we rest in the peace and assurance of our eternal destiny with God Himself (Rom. 6:22). This is a *positional* peace acquired "once and for all" through faith at the time of our salvation, and it is absolutely essential in "preparing" us to stand firm under enemy attack.

In addition to providing our salvation, the Gospel of Peace also serves as a powerful resource in our lives for experiencing a deep internal peace that is capable of sustaining us through the most difficult of circumstances here on earth (John 14:27; 16:33). Since the spiritual armor is something we are to "put on," I believe that appropriating this *experiential* peace is an equally important part of our protective footwear that "prepares" us to maintain our stability against the enemy. While it is always available to us, we determine the degree to which it characterizes our lives and hence the degree of spiritual protection it provides us (Isa. 26:3; Col. 3:15).

When we learn how to draw upon it, God's peace is a powerful antidote to the emotions of anger, anxiety, and fear, which make us particularly vulnerable to losing our grip spiritually and allowing Satan to gain a foothold in our lives (Gen. 4:6-7; Eph. 4:26). Strong emotions such as these can potentially overpower our mind's commitment to godliness, opening the door for our flesh to direct our actions instead. If we are to remain strong against the ploys of the enemy, we must become adept at exchanging these natural reactions to life's circumstances for God's incomprehensible peace (Phil. 4:7).

The first step is to become increasingly attuned to recognizing when our emotions have robbed us of peace. The quicker we catch ourselves and remedy the situation, the less time we will spend "bootless" on slippery terrain before our enemy.

Anger

Anger is a particularly volatile emotion which can erupt either as a natural response to a wrong suffered or as a fleshly reaction due to jealousy, envy, perfectionistic expectations, or selfish demands (Gal. 5:19-20). In either case anger puts us into an extremely vulnerable position spiritually with Satan "crouching at the door" and wooing us to succumb to his will (Gen. 4:5-7). God never condemns anger but strongly warns us not to allow our anger to lead us to commit sin or to become an ongoing bitterness in our lives (Eph. 4:26-27; James 1:20). Instead, He urges us to try to live in peace with all men (Rom. 14:19; Heb. 12:14-15).

When our anger arises from having been truly wronged by someone, the path to peace ultimately lies in forgiving the offender (Mark 11:25; Eph. 4:32) by relinquishing all desires for vengeance to God (Gen. 18:25; Rom. 12:19; Col. 3:25). Through forgiveness God allows us to rid ourselves of the emotional burden of determining and exacting the just fate of our offender by taking that responsibility on Himself. This generous act on His behalf enables us to experience peace and emotional health in spite of being grievously wronged. (See pp. 82-83 for a fuller description of the relationship between anger, hate, and forgiveness.)

When our anger stems from purely self-centered motives rather than from a true wrong being suffered, we need a major change in attitude. This can often be achieved by asking ourselves how God or another objective person would look at the situation. We must then decide if we are willing to give up our pride, jealousy, or perfectionistic demands. When we willfully choose to surrender these ungodly responses to God, His peace can once again replace our anger—and often defuse the external situation as well.

Anxiety

Anxiety is another natural emotional response that can easily disrupt our peace as we face the cares and chaos of this world. God does not promise to free us from such situations, but in the midst of the trials and troubles that will invariably come, He offers a supernatural oasis of peace for His children (John 16:33).

Experiencing this peace requires that we foster a dual awareness of both the physical and spiritual realms (2 Cor. 4:17-18; Col. 3:1-3). Anxieties increase if we focus only on the material realm and lose sight of all that transcends it. God's constant presence with us, the depth of His love, and the powerful resources He makes available to us are spiritual realities that make a major difference for the Christian when facing the challenges of life.

Securing God's supernatural peace also requires a deep knowledge of His Word (Ps. 119:65) so we can understand His character, His promises, and the nature of our relationship to Him. As these truths sink in, we will recognize that our loving Father, who abundantly provides for even the birds and flowers, will certainly care for His beloved children, who are of much greater value in His sight (Mat. 6:25-34; Phil. 4:19).

Nothing can ever separate us from His presence or His love (Ps. 139:1-12; Heb. 13:5; Rom. 8:38-39). He even promises that if we walk in love and obedience to Him, He will make every situation that befalls us somehow result in good (Gen. 50:20; Rom. 8:28). These are but a few of the unchangeable promises of God that form the bedrock foundation for the peace that He offers us in place of our anxieties (Heb. 6:17-19).

None of these truths can effect peace on its own, however. Peace only comes when we exercise our faith, believing God to be true to His Word, and *willfully relinquish* our anxieties (1 Peter 5:7). If we can truly rest secure in His love and sovereignty in even the direst of circumstances, He will give us His supernatural peace, which is so transforming that it defies understanding (Phil. 4:6-7).

Fear

Fear is another natural emotion that can quickly overtake us when our protective "antennae" sense any form of danger or we face situations which can potentially threaten our life, security, or well-being. The less control we have in determining our fate in such situations, the stronger the potential for fear. Whether the peril is real or imagined, anticipated or actually present, fear is a powerful emotion that can cripple our spiritual strength. Because of this Satan himself often works to instill or augment our fears.

Again, the supernatural peace of God can serve as an antidote for our fears in a way that unbelievers cannot possibly fathom (John 14:27). While experiencing this divine peace requires a major act of faith on our part, it is marvelously effective whether our fears concern the physical or spiritual realm; natural calamities, frightening circumstances, or threatening human beings.

Fear of Satan and demons. What is unseen can be particularly frightening, especially if it is perceived as evil. Perhaps this is one reason why many people, including some Christians, choose to live virtually oblivious to the spiritual realm—or at least the evil part of it. Some Christians have seemingly convinced themselves that demons exist only in the more heathen parts of the world or that if they ignore Satan and his forces, he too will ignore them. This is how they cope with the fear of unseen, supernatural, evil beings existing around them. This is tragic because denying the enemy leaves a person much more vulnerable to him.

Among those who accept the worldwide reality of demons, unbelievers do well to fear Satan and His demons. While some are intrigued by the supernatural abilities he seems to offer, this is totally deceptive as Satan has no intent of ever being beneficial to mankind. His object is to use man for his own ends. The truth is that Satan relates to those under his dominion as a master over his slaves, which should naturally evoke fear (Rom. 6:16; 8:15).

As children of God, however, we have been completely delivered from Satan's kingdom into God's kingdom through faith in the atoning blood of the Lord Jesus Christ (Col. 1:13), and God relates to those in His kingdom as a loving father to precious children (Rom 8:15). Because Satan moves from being our master to being our enemy when we enter God's family, he can still be an object of fear—but only to an ignorant believer.

When we clothe ourselves in the spiritual armor and use the authority which God has granted us in the spiritual realm, we can boldly command the obedience of Satan's forces in the powerful name of the Lord Jesus Christ (Luke 10:17; Acts 16:18; James 4:7). We need never cower before them. We have the means to be totally victorious over them—*if* we keep ourselves spiritually vigilant to recognize their attacks (I Pet. 5:8).

Fear of death and God's judgment. One of the most powerful fears mankind carries is the fear of death. Death is the punishment for sin that was established way back in the Garden of Eden and that is reiterated over and over again throughout Scripture (Gen. 2:16; 3:19, 22; Ezek. 18:4; Rom. 6:23, etc.). This death penalty would never have come upon man if Satan had not lured him into sin (Gen. 3:22). Therefore, Satan is said to hold the "power of death," and those who choose to remain under his dominion live their entire lives in bondage to the fear of death and the retribution for sin that lies beyond it (Heb. 2:14-15).

This fear is totally unnecessary for the child of God, however. When Jesus died on the Cross, He took upon Himself the punishment for our sins. *He suffered death in our place* (1 Pet. 3:18)! When we personally accept His substitutionary death for *our* sins, we are freed from the death penalty for our sins (John 3:16; 5:24; Rom. 8:1-2). While we will still die physically, we no longer have to *fear* death (Heb. 2:15). Its "sting" is removed (1 Cor. 15:55)! Death no longer leads to eternal punishment but rather to a glorious inheritance reserved in heaven for us (1 Pet. 1:4)!

John makes it quite clear that if we continue to live in fear of God's judgment, we do not understand the love of God that sent His Son to be the atoning sacrifice for our sins. As we fully grasp God's perfect love, which was demonstrated so clearly in this way, and allow this love to permeate our own lives, it totally banishes fear of punishment or judgment for our sins (1 John 4:7-21)! If God has justified us and Christ is interceding for us, what charge can possibly be brought against us (Rom. 8:33-34)?

Because the fear of death is such a powerful weapon in Satan's arsenal, he continues to try to use it against vulnerable Christians even though it has no validity in their lives. He seems to believe that pushing those in God's Kingdom to the point of death will cause them to relinquish their allegiance to God.

For this reason God repeatedly indicates through Scripture that to be effective in the work of His kingdom, Christians must be willing even to lay down their lives for the sake of the Gospel (1 John 3:16; Luke 14:26-27; Rev. 12:11). This need not be a fearsome thing, however, if we truly grasp the reality of God's love and the nature of our spiritual inheritance beyond the grave. By clinging to this faith, we can effectively exchange our natural fear in the face of death for God's inexplicable peace.

Fear of physical calamities. God's supernatural peace can supplant our fears in relationship to the natural realm as well as the spiritual realm. Once again our ability to secure that deep inner serenity in all circumstances depends on how deeply we understand and grasp the truths of Scripture concerning the nature of God and His promises (Ps. 119:165). Only by holding tightly to these can we, by faith, exchange our *natural* fears for His *supernatural* peace.

When we fully appropriate God's peace, we can say with the psalmist, "God is our refuge and strength, an ever-present help in trouble. Therefore, we will not fear, though the earth give way and the mountains fall into the heart of the sea, though its waters roar and foam and the mountains quake with their surging" (Ps. 46:1-3 NIV). Even terrifying physical calamities such as earthquakes, hurricanes, tornadoes, and floods occur within the scope of God's sovereignty. He is fully able to deliver us from all harm in the midst of these disasters if He chooses to do so (Mark 4:36-41; Ps. 91).

Our peace does not depend on God's protection, however. Our peace is based on the assurance that nothing can separate us from Him and His love—not even death (Rom. 8:38-39)! No matter how devastating a catastrophe threatens us, we know that God will either protect us from it, sustain us through it by His love and all-sufficient grace (2 Cor. 12:9; Heb. 4:16), or usher us victoriously into His presence (Ps. 23:4)! "*Whether we live or die, we belong to the Lord*" (Rom. 14:8)!

Fear of difficult circumstances. The reality of God's love, His promises, and His presence within us can carry us peacefully through frightening circumstances precipitated by human actions as well. Nothing that happens to us is ever out of God's sight or the scope of His sovereignty. He is aware of every detail of our lives and vitally concerned about each one (Ps. 31:14; 139:1-18; Mat. 10:29-31). *Resting by faith in the absolute security of our personal relationship to God as a loving Father* is the secret which enables us to have peace in a world filled with tribulation (Isa. 26:3; John 14:27; 16:33; Rom. 8:15).

While no circumstance is ever too difficult for God to overcome on our behalf (Jer. 32:17), He may sometimes choose to use potentially frightening or difficult situations to strengthen our faith in Him and develop our character (James 1:2-4; Rom. 5:3-4). Our faith can only grow when we confront situations that surpass what we can handle with our human capabilities alone. Only when we are thrust totally upon God can He prove His faithfulness to us, either by miraculously delivering us (2 Cor. 1:8-10) or by supernaturally equipping us to handle the trying situation (2 Cor. 3:5; 4:7; 12:9-10).

Even in these stretching experiences that God allows in our lives, however, we can experience supernatural peace as long as we keep our faith securely grounded in the reality of His love and His promise never to abandon us (Heb. 13:5-6). If we continue to reciprocate His love and walk obediently in His will, we can also be assured that whatever the situation is, God is working on our behalf to bring some benefit from it for ourselves. (Rom. 8:28). This is obviously easier to believe in hindsight when we see the results, but if we can exercise faith in this promise *during* the trial, it can be another means of enhancing our peace in difficult circumstances.

Fear of threatening people. Encountering people who seemingly have the power to hurt, humiliate, or take advantage of us in some way is another situation which naturally evokes fear. Again, however, God gives us the resources to overcome such fear and replace it with His supernatural peace.

Often this process begins by recognizing that we may be up against more than human dynamics in these situations. Although we know that God performs much of the work of His kingdom through the Holy Spirit indwelling and empowering His children, we often fail to recognize that Satan can work in a similar way through those in *his* kingdom, or even Christians who have allowed him to establish a stronghold in their lives. Therefore, what we may perceive as a human conflict may actually be propelled or augmented by demonic forces.

If this is the case, the fact that the Holy Spirit in us is greater than any of Satan's forces can greatly boost our confidence (1 John 4:4). We can often drastically change the nature of the conflict by doing simple spiritual warfare against the forces of darkness that may be operating in and through the other person and fueling the conflict. While we may not have the authority to cast demons out of another person who has given them a legal right to be there, as children of God, we do have the right to keep them from threatening or harming us.

Of course, we can't blame all human conflicts on the direct involvement of demons, but God has resources available to us when the dynamics are purely human as well. He reminded Timothy, when he was apparently fearful of persecution by those who were opposed to the Gospel message, that He has not given us "a spirit of timidity, but a spirit of **power**, of **love** and of **self-discipline**" (2 Tim. 1:7). This means that we can draw upon these divinely given capabilities that will somehow enable us to counteract our fears when dealing with hostile people.

Many Christians greatly underestimate the **power** that God makes available to those who have the faith to believe and claim it. Ephesians 1:19-21 says it is the same power that raised Jesus Christ from the dead and placed Him in a position of authority at the Father's right hand far above all created beings. Ephesians 3:20 says that God "is able to do immeasurably more than all we ask or imagine, according to his power that is at work within us."

This unfathomable outpouring of God's power into our lives is probably limited only by the degree of our ignorance, our arrogance, our lack of faith, or our failure to request it. Many of us are so accustomed to handling things with our own strength and abilities that we forget about the availability of God's power to help us. Whatever the reason, when we fail to draw upon God's power in challenging situations, we limit their outcome to that which can be obtained by human effort alone

When we are willing, however, to acknowledge our own inadequacies and surrender to the total sufficiency of God's enablement (2 Cor. 3:5), we open the door for His power to operate in and through us. In God's family when we are weak, then we are strong.

This principle enabled Paul to stand firmly in his Boots of Peace even when evil men insulted and persecuted him. He was confident that these were opportunities to see the power of God work marvelously on his behalf (2 Cor. 12:9-10). We too can stand in that same confidence—and peace!

In addition to His power, God gives us the resource of His divine **love** to fill and direct our lives (Rom. 5:5; 1 John 4:12). Love is another powerful spiritual "weapon," which can extinguish wrath, overcome evil, and bring conviction to our enemies (Prov. 15:1; Rom. 12:20). When we allow it to flow through our lives, it can transform our "people skills" so we are less likely to antagonize fearsome people and more apt to disarm them with a kind and gentle spirit (1 Cor. 13:4-7; Luke 6:27-28).

As we work for the Kingdom of God, we can naturally expect to encounter animosity (John 15:20). However, when God's love grips and motivates our hearts, our evangelistic zeal (2 Cor. 5:14-15) will supersede our fear of persecution, suffering, and humiliation, and we will willingly endure these for the cause of Christ (2 Tim. 1:7-8; Phil. 3:7-8).

Discipline is another dynamic which the Holy Spirit can enhance in our lives, enabling us to follow a consistent, committed lifestyle patterned after Christ Himself, regardless of the circumstances or the people confronting us (Gal. 5:22-23; Titus 2:11-12). Isaiah 32:17 says the fruit of such righteousness will be the inner experience of confidence and peace, giving us a firm foundation to stand on in confronting frightening people. Scripture clearly states that when our trust is in God, we need not fear what man can do to us (Ps. 27:1; 56:4; Heb. 13:5-6).

Through the abundant resources that God makes available to us, we can stand firmly in our Boots of Peace in any situation. Our success in doing so depends on our consistent awareness of His loving and powerful presence with us and the degree of faith we are willing to exercise in relinquishing our fears in exchange for God's peace. When we truly grasp "how wide and long and high and deep" is God's love for us and are filled with the fullness of His presence (Eph. 3:16-19), we have the antidote for all fear. How can we fear when He who is the epitome of love and power is living in us?

We are never out of God's sight, love, and sovereignty—no matter what situation we face, whether "trouble or hardship or persecution or famine or nakedness or danger or sword. . . . In all these things we are more than conquerors through Him who loved us" (Rom. 8:35-39; cf. Ps. 139:1-18). The "shadow of the Almighty" is always our place of refuge, and within it we find incredible security and peace (Ps. 91:1).

The Shield of Faith

"Faith is being sure of what we hope for and certain of what we do not see" (Heb. 11:1). It is not only the means through which we enter the Kingdom of God; it is the basis of the entire Christian life (Rom. 1:17; Gal. 2:20; 2 Cor. 5:7). It is also vitally important in our defense against the enemy. The stronger our faith and the more areas of life in which we exercise it, the more spiritual protection it provides.

Reinforcing the other Armor Pieces

Because faith is needed in so many aspects of the Christian life, it is aptly represented in the spiritual armor as the moveable shield, able to cover most any part of the body (Eph. 6:16). As the shield, faith supports and reinforces the effectiveness of the other pieces of the armor. In fact, putting on, maintaining, and using every other piece of the spiritual armor requires faith.

We receive the Helmet of Salvation as a gift from God by faith (Eph. 2:8). Having thus been transferred out of Satan's kingdom into God's family (Col. 1:13-14; Rom. 8:15), we can use our Shield of Faith to stand in firm assurance of our salvation whenever Satan flings crippling arrows of doubt at us (1 John 5:13).

The Shield of Faith also plays a major role in reinforcing the Breastplate of Righteousness. We accept and recognize the Holy Spirit's presence within us by faith (Gal 3:2). Tuning our hearts to hearing his "drumbeat" and allowing Him to direct our lives in righteousness instead of following the evil desires Satan has implanted in our flesh is also by faith (Gal. 5:16, 25).

Only by faith can we claim the reality of God's promises and keep our eyes focused on the magnitude of our inheritance in heaven so that the sinful allurements Satan has incorporated into our materialistic world will fade in importance and Satan will be unable to use these temptations to pierce our Breastplate of Righteousness (2 Cor. 4:17-18; 1 Peter 1:3-5; 2 Peter 1:4; 1 John 5:4). At those times when Satan is allowed by God to bring trials into our lives, faith enables us to maintain the integrity of our Breastplate of Righteousness, even when all sense of God's presence is obliterated (Job; James 1:2-4; Rom. 5:3-5; 2 Cor. 4:17; 5:7; Heb. 11:1; 1 Pet. 1:6-9).

Faith also reinforces the Belt of Truth in a number of ways. Through faith we believe the truths of Scripture and allow them to direct our lives (Ps. 119:11, 105; James 1:22-25; 2:14-26). By faith we also hold onto the conviction that God always honors truth, and we resist Satan's inner urgings to speak falsehood of any kind in any situation (Mat. 5:37; Ps. 24:3-5). Faith is also essential for proclaiming the powerful truths of Scripture to Satan's forces when under attack, melting them in their tracks (Mat. 4:1-11).

Only by faith can we put on, and stand firm in, our Boots of Peace, consistently allowing the peace of God to characterize our lives and relationships (Col. 3:15). Relinquishing our naturally occurring anger, anxiety, and fear and exchanging them for God's supernatural peace takes a tremendous act of faith, but it prevents these emotions from potentially becoming footholds for Satan to gain an advantage in our lives (Eph. 4:26-27).

Faith also keeps us aware of God's love and power and His unfailing presence with us, further diminishing fear and anxiety and enhancing peace in our lives (2 Cor. 12:9; 1 John 4:12). If we can hold tightly by faith to the security of our relationship to God as a loving Father (Rom. 8:15, 35-39), no situation in the natural or spiritual realm can rob us of God's peace (John 14:27; 16:33), not even the threat of death, which is one of the most powerful weapons in Satan's arsenal (Heb. 2:14-15; Rev. 12:11).

Learning to expect, rely upon, and recognize the internally spoken "Word of God" when confronting evil requires immense faith as well. Faith is equally necessary to take this "Word" as the powerful Sword of the Spirit and to speak it with confidence, even under persecution, trusting that God will use it in a mighty way to accomplish His purposes (Luke 21:12-15; Acts 13:8-12).

Evidence of Faith

Because our faith is so important in the spiritual battle, God deliberately works to build and strengthen it while Satan seeks to destroy it (2 Cor. 1:8-9; 1 Thes. 3:2-10; James 1:2-4; 1 Peter 1:6-7). The Book of Job dramatically reveals how God and Satan are pitted against each other in challenging and testing the strength of man's faith.

The measure of our faith does not lie in the degree to which we can perform miraculous deeds but rather in the extent to which it transforms our lives and actions (James 2:14-26). When we obey God's commandments, do His will, and follow the example of Jesus' life on earth, we are truly living out our faith (Mat. 7:15-23; 1 John 2:3-6). A vital, active faith in God always spawns a deep love for God and people, which is evident to those around us (Mat. 25:34-46; John 13:35; James 2:14-23: 1 John 4:20-21).

True faith not only transforms our lives, but it also unleashes within us the same power that raised Jesus Christ from the dead and placed Him in the position of supreme authority over all the powers of darkness (Eph. 1:19-23; Phil. 3:10). Because God graciously allows us, as His children, to share this position with Christ (Eph. 2:6), we can by faith use the authority of the name of Jesus to overcome Satan's forces too. Whenever we suspect that Satan may be attacking, intimidating, or taking advantage of us, we can boldly raise our **Shield of Faith** and resist him in the name of Jesus, and he will flee from us (Luke 10:17; Eph. 6:16; 1 Peter 5:8-9; James 4:7).

Faith in Prayer

Faith is also vitally important in maintaining effective communication with God. "Anyone who comes to Him must believe that He exists and that He rewards those who earnestly seek Him" (Heb. 11:6b). Since prayer is such a powerful lifeline giving us direct access to God and His awesome resources, Satan undoubtedly delights in seeing our faith in prayer diminish. Therefore, when our prayers seemingly go unanswered, we should not give in to despair but seek to understand why.

As we learn the criteria for effective prayer which God has revealed in Scripture, we will be able to pray much more knowledgeably. We will also understand the types of requests we can most expect God to answer, those He *may* choose to answer, and those we know He won't answer.

In John 14:13 Jesus told His disciples that He would do anything that they asked in His name so that He might bring glory to the Father. I believe that this promise holds two key principles concerning effective prayer.

The first essential element concerns the spiritual condition and motives our hearts as we come to God with our requests. This verse states that our prayers are to be made "in Jesus' name." Many Christians do this so glibly, totally missing the true significance of this directive. Praying in the name of Jesus means much more than tacking His name ritualistically onto the end of our prayers. God's solemn command not to misuse His name still bears relevance in our lives today (Ex. 20:7; Mat. 5:33-35) and must certainly apply to how we use it in prayer.

In biblical times one's name represented his complete identity or overall character,[1] somewhat similar to the authority of our signature today. Therefore, to live in blatant disregard of the character of Christ and yet to pray "in His name" dreadfully misuses it. We can only truly pray in the name of Jesus when our hearts are in line with His.[2] The model prayer which Jesus taught His disciples begins with such an expression of agreement with the will of God both in heaven and on earth (Mat. 6:10).

When we truly identify with the character, motivations, priorities, and desires of Jesus, we naturally fulfill the other requirements for effective prayer given throughout Scripture. For instance, we cannot align our hearts with Christ without confessing all known sin (James 5:16; 1 John 3:21-22), forgiving those who have wronged us (Mark 11:24-25), and allowing God's Word to be a living and active reality in our daily lives (John 15:7). Tuning our hearts to the heart of Christ will also bring our requests in line with His will (1 John 5:14-15) and strengthen our faith that God will truly answer them (James 1:6-8; Heb. 10:22; 11:6).

The second principle for effective prayer found in John 14:13 concerns the nature of the requests we bring to God. According to this passage they must be such that Jesus is able to bring glory to the Father by answering them.

Recognizing this as a critical criterion for effective prayer should motivate us to ascertain what brings glory to God. In the immediate context of this promise Jesus is speaking of those who have the faith *to continue His ministry on earth.* Certainly engaging in such activity would bring glory to the Father.

In John 15:16 Jesus similarly promises to answer the prayers of those who are *bearing fruit in the Kingdom of God.* Paul, too, indicates in 2 Thessalonians 1:11-12 that *walking worthy of God's calling, being devoted to "good" purposes,* and *allowing faith to manifest itself in good works in our lives* brings glory to the name of Christ. Therefore, we can legitimately expect God to answer prayers which are focused on the goal of continuing Jesus' ministry on earth and bearing fruit in His kingdom.

Paul's prayer in Philippians 1:9-11 reveals that our *growth in love, understanding, discernment, and righteousness* brings glory to God as well. Therefore, we can also confidently expect God to answer prayers for our own spiritual maturity.

Paul even prayed that God would give the Ephesian Christians "the Spirit of wisdom and revelation" and enlighten the "eyes of [their] heart" so that they would "know Him better" and fully comprehend the hope that is theirs, the glorious inheritance that they are to God, and the divine power available to those who believe (Eph. 1:17-19). According to this example, prayers for our spiritual growth can even include requests for God's supernatural revelation and enlightenment. Furthermore, we can ask for this not only for ourselves but for others as well.

James tells us of the trials that are bound to accompany the Christian's path to spiritual maturity, but in this context he also indicates that God is willing to answer all prayers for wisdom "without finding fault"—if our faith is unwavering (James 1:2-7). In this case the quality of our faith seemingly supercedes whatever "faults" may be in our lives. Perhaps the exercise of our faith brings glory to God in and of itself.

The Bible also gives repeated instructions or examples of believers praying for many other things, such as healing (James 5:14-16), relief from troubling circumstances (Phil. 4:6-7; James 5:13), protection (Neh. 4:6-9; Ezra 8:21-23; John 17:11-15), adversarial relationships (Ps. 6:6-10; Mat. 5:44; Luke 18:1-7), the welfare of one's country (Ps. 122:6; Jer. 29:7; 1 Tim. 2:1-2), the gift of children (1 Sam. 1:1-20), and the right marriage partner (Gen. 24). Therefore, we know that asking God to intervene in our personal areas of need is appropriate as well.

In bringing such requests to God, however, we must keep some important factors in mind. First of all, we must always remember that God's perspective is infinitely broader than ours and His plans wiser (Isa. 55:8-9). Therefore, if He does not answer one of these requests as we would like, we must believe that He is acting true to His character and with our best welfare in mind. This too requires faith. Sometimes God allows difficult circumstances in our lives to increase our faith or to build our character, viewing these goals as higher priorities.

Secondly, God will not violate the free will of any individual. Therefore, when another person's will is involved in a request we make, praying that God will bring into that person's life the people, the circumstances, and the resources which might motivate him to respond in a specified manner may be more fruitful. Even then, however, we cannot automatically expect God to bring the outcome we desire.

Thirdly, God has established natural and spiritual laws by which He normally intends His creation to operate. Therefore, when we ask Him to intervene on our behalf and override these divinely instituted principles, He is never *obligated* to do so; nor do we ever *deserve* such a response. If He chooses to intervene on our behalf, He does so as an extension of His grace. That He is *willing* to do this is clearly evidenced in Hebrews 4:16, however, as He invites us to come boldly before His throne to receive His grace and mercy in our times of need.

Other passages indicate that the degree of our faith and the persistence of our prayers may serve to influence God's response to our requests regarding personal needs (Mat. 15:21-28; Mark 11:24; Luke 11:5-10). God's admonition concerning prayer immediately following His description of the spiritual armor (Eph. 6:18) seems to imply that spiritual warfare may also be needed in the context of prayer. This is clearly illustrated in Daniel 10:1-14. At times fasting can seemingly have a positive effect as well (Mat. 6:16-18; Luke 2:37; Acts 14:23).

Finally, we must also remember that God created us to have a reciprocal love relationship with Himself and that He actively competes with Satan for our devotion. As any jealous suitor, God will never answer prayers that arise from our fleshly nature, which is warped by Satan to seek self-gratification, or that will draw us closer to the world system, which is also under Satan's control (James 4:3-5; 1 John 2:15-17; 5:19).

As any loving father, however, God is eager to give good gifts to His children, even beyond what we ask—sometimes even beyond our greatest imaginations (Matt. 7:9-11; Eph. 3:20; James 1:17; Ps. 84:11). When our hearts genuinely delight in Him, Scripture says that He will graciously and lovingly fulfill the desires of our hearts (Ps. 37:4). What a Father! Praise His holy name!

The Helmet of Salvation

A soldier entering a military battle without a helmet would be considered insane. The head is one of the most critical areas to protect as it houses the vital control center of the entire body. Entering a spiritual battle without the Helmet of Salvation is just as dangerous. Scripture vividly recounts that when the unsaved sons of Sceva attempted to cast out a demon in the name of Jesus, they were overpowered and beaten so badly that they "ran out of the house naked and bleeding" (Acts 19:13-16). Apart from our personal salvation through the blood of Jesus Christ, we have no basis for overcoming the evil one.

When Jesus shed His blood on the Cross to effect our salvation, in some glorious and final way He disarmed and triumphed over all demonic powers and authorities (Col. 2:15). God then seated the risen Christ at His own right hand in an everlasting position of authority far above all ruling powers, both human and spiritual (Eph. 1:19-21). This side of heaven we will never fully comprehend the enormity of the dynamics which transpired in the spiritual realm through Christ's death, burial, and resurrection. Through salvation, however, the awesome power of these events is applied to our own lives.

While Jesus died for the sins of the whole world, we must *individually* accept His death as the full payment for *our* sins (John 1:12; 3:16-18). This act of faith translates us out of Satan's dominion into the Kingdom of God (Col. 1:13) and seats us *with Christ* in the heavenly realm, enabling us to share His authority over the forces of darkness (Eph. 2:6). What grace and mercy He extends to us! What awesome stature He gives to His children in the spiritual realm! What can possibly compare to love of this magnitude?

In this marvelous position we also enjoy the permanent, protective covering of the blood of Jesus. Represented by the Helmet of Salvation, this covering assures us that Satan can never render a fatal blow to the spiritual life Christ has secured for us.

Because of the foundational role that salvation plays in our defense against Satan, we might expect the Helmet of Salvation to be listed first among the pieces of the armor. Instead, it is almost the last piece mentioned.

Rather than reflecting a lack of importance, however, its placement near the end of the list may be more indicative of its low maintenance requirement. Unlike the other parts of the spiritual armor, putting on the Helmet of Salvation does not require daily vigilance or effort on our part. The Helmet of Salvation is given to us as a *gift* from God. This difference is not only consistent with the rest of Scripture (Rom. 6:23; Eph. 2:8) but is also indicated by the Greek word translated "take" in this verse.[3] How gracious of God to make the most vital part of our spiritual protection depend not on our efforts but on His free and everlasting gift to us!

The Sword of the Spirit

The Sword of the Spirit is the only offensive weapon included in the spiritual armor. Like the Helmet of Salvation, it too is given as a gift from God.[4] In this case, however, rather than being given "once and for all" as a permanent inheritance, the Sword of the Spirit is repeatedly provided whenever God considers it to be needed. Our responsibility is to learn to rely on its availability and not to grasp for our own fleshly wisdom when confronting the enemy.

While the Sword of the Spirit is quickly identified as the "Word of God," the Greek word used (*rhema*) refers specifically to the *spoken* Word of God.[5] This means that at certain critical times God promises to give us the words that will effectively counteract the assault of the enemy or enable us to share the gospel message while under extreme persecution or duress.

God's intent is that the Sword of the Spirit not only strike with supernatural power but also free us from anxiety over choosing our own words at those adrenaline pumping times (Mat. 10:16-20). The Sword of the Spirit is thus another resource graciously given by God to enable us to maintain the firm grip of our Boots of Peace as well.

Whether we stand before rulers for the sake of the Gospel or confront demonized individuals (Acts 13:6-12), we must learn to be sensitive to the inner voice of the Holy Spirit and boldly deliver the words He gives us. When we do, we can be assured that those divinely chosen words will be such that "none of [our] adversaries will be able to resist or contradict" them (Luke 21:15).

Conclusion

Keeping adequately protected against the spiritual attacks that Satan and his forces may launch against us requires a close partnership with God. It is only possible if we have by faith accepted and applied the reality of Jesus' substitutionary death on the Cross to our *own* sins and are thereby delivered from Satan's kingdom into God's. At this point God freely gives us the Helmet of Salvation and makes His divine resources available to us. He also stands ready to give us the Sword of the Spirit whenever we need divinely powerful words to confront Satan and his work in whatever form that might take.

Beyond this, we are responsible for keeping the other pieces of the spiritual armor firmly in place, drawing upon the totally sufficient resources which God supplies. This requires exercising an ever-increasing faith in His unfailing love and presence with us, becoming sensitive to the realities of the spiritual realm, and committing ourselves to live according to God's righteous standards laid down in Scripture for us. When our lives are consistently characterized by truth, righteousness, peace, and faith, the arrows Satan aims at us will find no resting place.

Endnotes

[1] *The NIV Study Bible* (Grand Rapids: Zondervan, 1995); note on John 2:23.

[2] Ibid.; note on John 14:13.

[3] *The Ryrie Study Bible: New American Standard Translation* (Chicago: Moody, 1978), note on Ephesians 6:17.

[4] Ibid.

[5] John F. Walvoord and Roy B. Zuck, eds., *The Bible Knowledge Commentary* (Wheaton, IL: Scripture Press, 1983, 1985).

Appendices

Appendix A

Definition of Terms

ABREACTION—The recall of a traumatic memory in such vivid sensory and affective form that it seems like a re-experiencing of the event.

ACCESS (verb)—To make direct or indirect contact with a programmed cult member through physical, electronic, or possibly spiritual means; may involve predetermined signals or programmed triggers.

ACTING OUT—Demonstrating unhealthy, non-productive behavior related to one's unresolved psychological issues.

AFFECT (noun)—A psychological term referring to emotions or the facial expression of emotions.

ALTER—An abbreviated form of "alternate personality" or "alternate identity."

ALTER-IDENTITY—A part of the person's soul that is separated by dissociation from the Core identity; often used interchangeably with "alter-personality" but technically may, or may not, have a completely developed personality of its own.

ALTER-PERSONALITY—A part of the person's soul that is separated by dissociation from the Core identity and has a relatively enduring pattern of perceiving, thinking about, and relating to self, others, and the environment.

ALTERED STATE OF CONSCIOUSNESS—Any shift of the focus of one's attention away from a clear connectedness to the immediate external environment.

AMNESIA—The inability to recall significant events or other important information which is too extreme to be explained by ordinary forgetfulness; the absence of memory.

BODY MEMORY—The re-experiencing of the pain or physical sensations of a past traumatic event or the re-appearance of bruises, marks, or wounds on the body from such an event.

BLACKOUT—A loss of consciousness experienced by a particular identity while another identity is in executive control of the body.

CO-CONSCIOUSNESS—The phenomenon of more than one identity sharing an awareness of external life at the same time; usually refers to the Host maintaining an awareness of events which transpire when other identities take executive control of the body.

CONDITIONING—The process by which a consistent behavioral pattern is established in response to a given stimulus.

CORE—The identity which represents the original, whole person conceived in the womb; carries the strongest sense of "self"; used synonymously with "Core Self," the "Original Self," or "Original Person"; sometimes used to refer to the identity who, among all those currently participating in life, is most directly related to the Original Self.

CORE SPLIT—A first generation alter-personality dissociatively separated directly from the Core.

COVERT—Hidden, secret, undeclared or unrevealed.

CULT—An organized group of people devoted to beliefs and goals which are not held by the majority of society; often religious in nature; in this book used to refer to an organized, covert perpetrator group.

CULTIST—Any perpetrator who is part of an organized group of people devoted to a specific covert agenda not shared by the general population.

DARKNESS—Referring to Satan's realm; usually associated with evil and deception.

DECOMPENSATION—Loss of psychological or functional stability.

DELIVERANCE—The process of freeing a person or identity (in DID) from demonization.

DEMON—An evil spirit associated with Satan and his agenda.

DEMONIZATION—The association of one or more specific demons with an individual (or alter) resulting in varying degrees of control or influence over the person (or alter).

DISSOCIATE—To separate all or part of one's consciousness from awareness of the physical environment; in DID, to split off part of one's soul into a separate identity or to switch from one identity to another.

DISSOCIATION—A temporary or prolonged disruption in normal consciousness in which one's sense of identity, memory, and/or perception of the environment may be altered or separated. This phenomenon lies on a continuum ranging from normal day-dreaming and "highway hypnosis" on one end to the formation of distinct, enduring alternate-identities (DID) at the other end.

DISSOCIATIVE—Having an increased propensity for dissociation, i.e., separating all or part of one's consciousness from awareness of the external environment; includes, but is not limited to, those with DID.

DISSOCIATIVE IDENTITY DISORDER (DID)—The new official term for what was formerly known as Multiple Personality Disorder; the psychological phenomenon of having two or more distinct, enduring identities within a single person, each demonstrating a consistent perspective of, and pattern of relating to, self, others, and environment, with at least two of them recurrently taking executive control of the person's behavior.

EXECUTIVE CONTROL—The ability to determine the actions of the body.

FOOTHOLD—The legal ground that gives a demon the right to become associated with and influence a person or identity. This could be an oath, vow, pledge that was made; a ritual or sacrifice participated in; a generational inheritance; or a specific sin or pattern of sinful behavior established in a person's life.

FRAGMENT—An alter-identity with a limited life history and function that does not have a fully developed personality.

FUSION—The merging of two alter-identities so that they become one. Technically this reversal of the dissociation process is differentiated from "integration" in that neither of the merging identities is the Core.

GENEALOGICAL MAP—A flow-chart showing the derivation of the alter-identities as they progressively split off from the Core or other identities.

GENERATIONAL SATANISM—Satanism which is propagated through succeeding generations.

HOST—The presenter personality who is most often in executive control of the body. (This can change over the course of the individual's life.)

IDENTITY—A person's distinct sense of self; used in DID to refer to each divided part of the soul created by dissociation; is sometimes used interchangeably with "alter" or "personality" but technically may, or may not, have a completely developed personality.

INNER SELF HELPER (ISH)—An alter-identity who is devoted to the good of the person and works to maintain internal stability and well-being; may provide helpful information to guide the therapist; rarely participates in external life.

INNER WORLD—A seemingly internal realm of mental imagery, often representing the system map, where some identities may interact with each other when they are not participating in external life. Sometimes this alternate level of consciousness can seemingly intersect with the spiritual realm, enabling the visualization of interaction between alters and demons.

INTEGRATION—The process of joining alter-identities back into the Core Self; a reversal of dissociation.

LAYER—A group of alters who are loosely related and aware of each other and may have participated in life together at one time. Multiple layers of alters usually exist in a system beneath the current group of presenters. In survivors of ritual abuse these are often strategically positioned to reinforce the programming and provide additional defenses against therapeutic intrusions.

LOSS OF TIME—The phenomenon of time passing for which the Host or a particular alter-identity is amnesic.

MULTIPLE—A person who has been diagnosed with Dissociative Identity Disorder, having more than one identity.

MULTIPLE PERSONALITY DISORDER (MPD)—The former title for the psychological diagnosis now known as "Dissociative Identity Disorder."

ORIGINAL SELF—The person created at conception from which the first alter-identities were split; often used synonymously with "Core."

OCCULT—Hidden or secret; often involving evil, supernatural powers or a secret knowledge of them.

"OUT"—Participating in external life.

PERPETRATOR—A person who abuses another person.

PERSONALITY—A relatively enduring pattern of perceiving and relating to self, others, and the environment. In DID it can refer to any identity exhibiting such a pattern.

PRESENT (verb)—To emerge into external consciousness and take part in life.

PRESENTER—An identity who consistently plays a role in normal daily living, usually having little or no knowledge of the abuse.

PRESENTER SYSTEM—The group of identities that normally handles daily life for the person.

PRIMARY IDENTITY—Any of several identities who carry the strongest investment in the Core's beliefs and commitments as well as in the dissociative barriers necessary to maintain them; includes the Core and a limited number of directly related identities, usually including the Host.

PROGRAM—A predetermined response pattern deliberately established in a person's mind to occur automatically when triggered by a specific stimulus.

PROGRAMMING—The entire conglomerate of programs established in a person's mind by a perpetrator group to direct behavior, thoughts, emotions, and/or the withholding of information, deliberately designed to establish partial or complete control over the individual.

RITUAL ABUSE—A systematic form of abuse having a predetermined purpose or agenda, usually involving the deliberate use of trauma to induce dissociation and some form of mind control programming; includes what has been known as Satanic Ritual Abuse (SRA).

SATANIC CULT—An organized group of people with an established belief system involving the direct or indirect worship of Satan and/or evil celestial beings and the seeking and exercising of occult powers.

SATANIC RITUAL ABUSE (SRA)—Severe trauma/torture experienced at the hands of a Satanic cult to cause dissociation into multiple identities so that some of those identities can be indoctrinated, programmed, and demonized, bringing the individual significantly under the control of the cult and the kingdom of darkness, generally without the knowledge of the Host personality.

SPIRITUAL WARFARE—The utilization of spiritual principles which apply the authority of the name and the shed blood of the Lord Jesus Christ to counteract demonic activity.

SPLIT—To form an alter-identity through dissociation.

SURVIVOR—A person who has been severely abused; a preferred term to "victim."

SWITCH—To change the executive control of the body from one identity to another in a person with DID.

SYSTEM—The entire group of identities within an individual who has Dissociative Identity Disorder; can also be used of a sub-group of identities with a distinct authority structure which functions more or less independently within the whole.

SYSTEM MAP—An internal mental imagery depiction of the structural arrangement and operational dynamics of all the identities in the system, providing a line of authority and a method of presentation or participation in life. The type of imagery used varies greatly (a house, a castle, a solar system, a carousel, a forest, etc.) and is usually distinct for every multiple.

TALK THROUGH—The process by which a therapist (or other person) addresses alters who are not in control of the body or willing to acknowledge their presence but are able to listen to what is said.

TRIGGER (noun)—A specific stimulus which consistently causes a given response; may be one which is deliberately designed to activate an established program.

TRIGGER (verb)—To cause a specific response, especially a consistent or programmed response.

Appendix B

Types of Alter-Identities

CORE—The identity who represents the whole person conceived in the womb; carries the strongest sense of "self"; may be called "Original Self" or "Original Person."

***HOST**—The presenter personality who is in executive control of the body most of the time, often is directly related to the Core.

***PRESENTERS**—The group of identities that normally handles daily living; includes the Host.

FUNCTION ALTERS—Alters created to perform specific functions unhindered by the effects of the trauma or to "protect" certain talents or encapsulate certain emotions, positive or negative; often serve as presenters.

VICTIMS—Alters whose sole function was to handle trauma.

CARETAKER—An alter who watches over, and may speak for, very young alters.

PROTECTORS—Alters created to protect the person or specific alters from any perceived danger and/or further abuse; may intervene to take abuse in place of weaker alters; often carry a lot of anger and can be aggressive.

INNER SELF HELPER (ISH)—An internal alter who is devoted to the good of the person and works to maintain internal stability and well-being; often provides helpful information to guide the therapist.

REPORTER—An alter who serves to keep track of the facts and relate them without emotion; may also be called "narrator," "moderator," "historian," etc.

CONTROLLERS—Alters who determine which alter will come out at a given time to handle a given situation.

PERSECUTORS—Alters who have identified with the motives and agenda of the abuser and punish the other alters, internally or externally, in the absence of the abuser when the alters do not perform as desired.

SHELL—An alter through whom the personalities and perspectives of other alters can present. This "hand-in-glove" type of presentation serves to maintain a sense of ongoing, consistent identity outwardly and a continuous short-term memory for the individual, thus minimizing the sense of time loss and the appearance of switching. While the shell functions as the speaker, it usually has no developed personality of its own. Sometimes a shell may serve solely to provide "housing" for a demon, which can then express itself through a human voice.

CULT ALTERS—Alters who participate(d) in cult activities, exhibiting varying degrees of cult loyalty. This general group of alters includes victims, protectors, persecutors, and reporters. In this case, protectors serve to guard cult secrets and critical parts of the system, block therapy, and/or warn the internal system or cult of any threat to its agenda. Reporters relate the activities of the person back to the cult.

* These can change over the course of a person's life.

Appendix C[1]

Satanic Calendar

Date	Event	Rituals
January 7	*St. Winebald's Day*	Blood Rituals
January 17	*Satanic Revels*	Sexual Rituals
*January 20-26	*Sacrificial Preparation for Grand Climax*	
*January 27	*Grand Climax*	Sexual Rituals & Human Sacrifice
February 2	*Candlemas (Sabbat Festival)*	Blood Rituals
February 25	*St. Walpurgis Day*	Blood Rituals
March 1	*St. Eichatadt Day*	Blood Rituals
*March 20/21	*Spring Equinox Feast Day (Sabbat Festival)*	Sexual Rituals
March 21	*Ostara*	Sexual Rituals
*Good Friday	*Day of Passion*	Human Sacrifice
*Easter Eve Day		Human Sacrifice
*April 21-25	*Sacrificial Preparation for Grand Climax*	
*April 26	*Grand Climax*	Sexual & Blood Rituals
April 30	*Roodmas Day, Walpurgis Night*	Sexual & Blood Rituals
May 1	*Beltane, Walpurgis Day Druid Fire Festival*	Coven Initiations
*June 21	*Summer Solstice Feast*	Sexual & Blood Rituals
July 1	*Demon Revels*	Blood Rituals Sexual Rituals with Demons
*July 20-26	*Sacrificial Preparation for Grand Climax*	
*July 27	*Grand Climax*	Sexual Rituals & Human Sacrifice
July 31 or August 1	*Lammas Day (Sabbat Festival)*	Sexual & Blood Rituals
August 1	*Lughnasadh*	Sexual Rituals
August 3	*Satanic Revels*	Sexual Rituals
September 7	*Marriage to the Beast*	Sexual Rituals & Infant Sacrifice
September 20	*Midnight Host*	Blood Rituals (Hand of Glory)

September 22	*Autumnal Equinox Feast Day*	Sexual Rituals
October 28	*Satanist High Holy Day*	Human Sacrifices
October 29	*Satanist High Holy Day*	Human Sacrifices
October 30	*Satanist High Holy Day*	Human Sacrifices
October 31	*All Hallows Eve (Samhain)*	Blood & Sexual Rituals with Demons
November 1	*Satanist High Holy Day*	Sexual Rituals & Human Sacrifices
November 4	*Satanic Revels*	Sexual Rituals
December 22	*Winter Solstice Feast Day (Sabbat Festival)*	Sexual Rituals
December 24	*Demon Revels, High Grand Climax*	Blood Rituals

Each New Moon	Blood Rituals
Each Full Moon *Esbat*	Blood & Sexual Rituals
*Birthdays of members	
*Birthday of high priest	

The Feast of the Beast occurs every 28 years. Last occurred in 1981. Next one is due in 2009.

Note: Most feast days begin either at sunset the evening before or at the stroke of midnight.

*Denotes most important dates

Endnote

[1] "America's Best Kept Secret," *Passport* Magazine, 1987.